What Readers Are Saying

"Steve's book was not only witty and well written, but so affirming, encouraging, and engaging that, before I knew it, I'd reached the end during one short, sunny afternoon sitting. He outlines fundamental principles applicable to any relationship, while providing clear biblical direction for singles all over the world. I've already started sharing the book with others!" **Lisa (USA)**

"I've finished your book. It was really interesting. Thank you for writing in simple words and nice sentences. It was easy to read and understand, even for me who has poor English experience. I am 35 years old, and still single. I was married, but was divorced 10 years ago. I have met some guys so far, but still single though. Ha, ha, ha! I try to improve my love and compassion, and wait for one day to meet someone who will have the same soul as me. Thank you very much again for giving a great time with your book!!" **Yuki (Japan)**

"I just read your book Secure In An Insecure World*, and I liked it very much. A lot of wisdom and great insights! I got married this summer to Natasha from Kiev, and she gave me this book when she went on a book search in a Christian bookstore here in Kiev. So the content of the book is very relevant. I am from Norway, and I love fishing and running."* **Havard (Norway)**

"Your book made me more intelligent and encouraged me a lot!!! Sure, I am just 18 and I am not in a hurry to get married, but as every human being, I think, pray and dream about this moment! I have 3 girlfriends, and they are in a queue to read your book, so I think that this book will be used a lot!!!" **Rusya (Ukraine)**

"I finished reading your book, and it really encouraged me. I've been praying for some time now that the Lord would teach/remind me how He loves me, and He has certainly answered my prayers, and filled me up so I can continue to love others with His love. I feel more freedom from my worries about marriage than I ever remember. Thanks for sharing the truth so concisely. I have been encouraging a lot of people to read your book, I actually think that it is a book that every young single should read, as well as most likely every young couple." **Corrie (USA)**

"Steve, finally I received your book — thank you so much, I can't stop reading it. It is amazing, it is truly a good piece. It is as if I am sitting and listening to you... very much your style and for the Lord's glory!" **Katia (UK)**

"Steve Nelson's book is very easy to read and understand. It lays out principles that have great importance for building a strong marriage. I am confident that this book will be useful both for those who will get married, and for those who have been married many years, but for some reason don't have complete joy in their relationship." **Dmitry (Ukraine)**

"We got the book on Saturday. I read it yesterday and gave it to my daughter this morning. The book is so good, and so well written. It is just as relevant for someone my age, with 26 years of marriage as it is for my daughters 20 and 25 years old." **Pam (USA)**

"I decided to buy it in order to prepare myself for my forthcoming wedding but, I realized that this book is really not only for people who are about to get married but it's great for everybody. It was like a bucket of cold water in the face, telling me: 'Make sure you don't believe the lies this world tells you about feeling secure, fulfilled and happy, but seek God and he will give you real contentment'. I also appreciated the 7 suggestions to a couple, it's always important to have some clear, practical steps to follow." **Andrea (Italy)**

"Your book <u>Secure in an Insecure World</u> is blowing me away... I am 51 years old and feeling so lonely, getting ready to celebrate our 25th wedding anniversary. My coworker shared your book with me. What is crazy about receiving this book is that someone in Sweden sent it to her, someone she doesn't even know. She read it and then shared it with me. I knew I had issues, but I didn't know it was insecurity. It made such sense and it was what the Father is telling me... "Take time to seek ME." Great book to help me focus on the Father! Please let me know how I can order this book!!!!! I will need at least 4 copies (1 for each of my kids) because what I'm reading in your book will help my single children find a fulfilling relationship with God and then have a wonderful marriage...

3

I knew God as savior, but was living my parent's faith. This way they will be given the tools to have a relationship with the Father and know that this is the relationship they are truly searching for." **Carol (USA)**

"Thank you very much for your book, I really enjoyed reading it! One of our friends is reading your book too and she says that it made her realize that she is not ready for relationships with guys. We have to find peace, security and contentment in God and not to look for those things in other people! Thank you very much for sharing your experience! Have you thought about writing one more book? :)" **Marina (Ukraine)**

"My husband left me and we were divorced this year. In the depths of my heart, I would like to be re-married, but am leaving the choice and timing in God's all-sufficient hands. I praise God that He alone is my Husband and I thank Him for doing a mighty work in my heart. I have told a friend how wonderful I think your book is! I have underlined quite a bit of it and now want to re-read it with my yellow highlighter handy. I think it should be "required" reading for any singles these days." **Amy (USA)**

"I like the book, because it is full of insights and practical help. I agree with everything that is written. My hope is, that especially the unmarried readers take the advice seriously, are patient and trust that God's plan for them is the best. I am so thankful that He gave me the perfect spouse 15 years ago. It is worth to wait for God's Mrs. Right!" **Oliver (Germany)**

SECURE
IN AN
INSECURE WORLD

Finding the Love
of Your Life

Stephen Scott Nelson

Secure In An Insecure World

Published by Phoenix Publishing. Kiev, Ukraine

ISBN 978-966-651-690-2

Acknowledgements

This book was a labor of love.
My heartfelt thanks go to my family and friends for
their help in editing — numerous times! Thank you,
Stopa Mihaylov, for your creative drawings and
excellent layout. Thank you to everyone who prayed
and encouraged me to write this book.

Danelle, my sweetheart, wife and best friend,
thank you for your faithful
support and hard work.

Most of all I thank my God
for making me secure in His love so that I
would even attempt this project.
He gets all the praise!

Contents

Prelude 11

Introduction 13

Chapter 1 — I've Got My Man! 17

Chapter 1 Discussion Questions 25

Chapter 2— Love — What Is It Really? 27

Chapter 2 Discussion Questions 44

Chapter 3— Quick and Easy 45

Chapter 3 Discussion Questions 63

Chapter 4 -How Did I Get This Way? 65

Chapter 4 Discussion Questions 79

Chapter 5 -Is Contentment Possible? 81

Chapter 5 Discussion Questions 99

Chapter 6— Why Get Married? 101

Chapter 6 Discussion Questions 114

Chapter 7 -Should I Consider Remarriage? 115

Chapter 7 Discussion Questions 124

Chapter 8 -Becoming Secure 125

Chapter 8 Discussion Questions 143

Chapter 9-Finding the Right One 145

Chapter 9 Discussion Questions 169

Chapter 10 — Receiving Life from God 171

Marriage Covenants 175

Chapter 10 Discussion Questions 179

Notes 181

Prelude

For many years I have been concerned about the needs of singles challenged by the decision of who to marry. This has been accentuated by my living in Kiev, Ukraine for the past four years. In Ukraine there is a stigma attached to being single past the age of twenty-five, especially if you are a woman. Choosing a marriage partner is one of life's major decisions, and sadly, we often fail miserably at it, and don't even know why. I wrote this book for teens, twenty and thirty year olds, divorcees, or in other words, everyone! We are all born with tremendous insecurities. Our upbringing can compound these natural deficiencies. Henry David Thoreau said, "Most men lead lives of quiet desperation." When we are desperate, this "quiet desperation" will lead us to make foolish decisions that can result in a great amount of pain and regret. My goal is to help you understand why you do what you do, and how you can make positive changes. The purpose of this undertaking is for you to understand your insecurities and discover where true security is found. The quiet desperation can be overcome! If you make this huge step, you will operate your life from a position of strength, leading to a wise decision regarding your marriage partner. In fact, every decision you make, from what career you choose to how you dress, will be affected by this new outlook on life! Your new found security will also drastically improve your relationship with your spouse as well as your parents, children, teachers, boss, employees and friends.

Please understand, this is not a self-help book leading you through steps to find a marriage partner. Your life's path may be to remain single, because that is where you will be the most satisfied. That said, most people will get married. Either way, the truths of this book will prepare you for these decisions. My heart's desire is for you to be truly secure in the journey.

Helen Keller, the legendary blind and deaf author, said, "Security is mostly a matter of superstition. It does not exist in nature, nor do humans usually experience it. Avoiding the danger is not safer in the long run than exposure. Life is either a daring adventure or nothing."

Actually, I am convinced that security *is* possible for every human! Not by avoiding the danger, but by understanding it and learning the source of real security. Are you ready to begin the daring adventure?

Yours in the adventure we call life,

Steve Nelson
Kiev, Ukraine

Introduction

True peace and security is what every human soul longs for, but we find it difficult to describe this yearning. This anonymous story illustrates these universal longings as well as anything I have ever read.

One day an artist was commissioned by a wealthy man to paint something that would depict peace. After a great deal of thought, the artist painted a beautiful country scene. There were green fields with cows standing in them, birds were flying in the blue sky and a lovely little village lay in a distant valley. The artist gave the finished painting to the man, but there was a look of disappointment on the patron's face. The man said to the artist, "This isn't a picture of true peace. It isn't right. Go back and try again."

The artist went back to his studio, thought for several hours about peace, then went to his canvas and began to paint. When he was finished, there on the canvas was a beautiful picture of a mother, holding a sleeping baby in her arms, smiling lovingly at her child. He thought, surely, this is true peace, and hurried to give the picture to the wealthy man. But again, the wealthy man refused the painting and asked the painter to try again.

The artist returned again to his studio. He was discouraged, he was tired, and he was disappointed. Anger swelled inside him as he felt rejection from the wealthy man. Again, he contemplated the possibilities, he even prayed for inspiration to paint a picture of true peace. Then, all of a sudden an idea came to him. He rushed to the canvas and began to paint as he had never painted before. When he finished, he hurried to show the wealthy man his creation. He gave him the painting and watched as he studied it carefully for several minutes. The artist held his breath. Then the wealthy man said, "Now *this* is a picture of true peace." He accepted the painting, paid the artist and everyone was happy.

And what was this picture of true peace? It showed a stormy sea pounding against a rock cliff. The artist had captured the fury of the wind, and the menacing black rain clouds laced with streaks of lightening. The sea was roaring in turmoil as the waves were churning and crashing upon the rocks. The dark sky was filled with the power of the furious thunderstorm. And, in the middle of the picture, under a cliff, the artist had painted a small bird with her young, safe and dry in their nest. The bird was at peace amidst the storm that raged around her.

We are going to embark on an adventure to discover true peace and security that most people believe is found only in a painting or in a fairy tale. But it is not — it is real! Finding this security will prepare you for choosing your marriage partner. It will prepare you to live life to the fullest. You must search and find it. Your life and your potential marriage are worth the effort!

Chapter 1

The knot in my stomach was only surpassed by the haunting doubts in my mind. Was it true? Had I walked into class, only to discover it was time for the final exam and I hadn't attended class all semester? My nausea also affirmed the truth that I had never even cracked a book for the class and my graduation depended on it!

Many of us have had this recurring nightmare after graduating from high school or college. We were terrified because we were totally unprepared. I hate having that dream! Singles faced with the decision of who to marry are often similarly unprepared for this major decision. Anyone can find a marriage partner. The question is, "Are you prepared to find the right person, and for the right reasons?"

This reminds me of one college student who "got her man." It was a hot, humid day in Columbia, SC on the University of South Carolina (USC) campus, typical early fall weather for the southeastern United States.

That day I was speaking to a group of students and was excited by the positive response. Even though I felt like a chicken roasting on the grill, as I perspired in the hot sunshine, the humid weather had not wilted my spirits. The interaction with the students on important issues energized me. "Sex, Love and Marriage" is one topic that is always popular with college students. I remember how thoughts of the opposite sex constantly crossed my mind when I was in college. Today many students were asking me sincere questions about this topic and we enjoyed a lively debate.

The Greek philosopher Socrates said, "The unexamined life is not worth living." I wholeheartedly agree with old Socrates! Why do most of us never take the time to seriously examine our lives? Is it that we don't like the potential answers? Maybe we don't believe that significant change is actually possible for us. Have we made attempts to change and become disillusioned with our paltry results? This is why I thoroughly enjoy interacting with college students, answering their questions, watching them think critically, and examine the important issues of life. For the past thirty years I have worked on college campuses with students who are seeking answers to these questions. Most students believe change is possible and they are idealistic enough to make the attempt. They have not become cynical, not yet. Many are on the verge of answering the major questions of life, "Who will I marry?" "What is my purpose in life?" On this particular day, we were discussing genuine love and how to know who to marry.

Socrates said,
"The unexamined life
is not worth living."

When I finished speaking with the crowd, a young coed named Sharon approached me and began expounding the virtues of her new lover. She enthusiastically told me, with great conviction, that she had found her soul mate just a few weeks ago. "I know that Mark is the one I will marry!" she said, overflowing with delight and anticipation. Sharon continued, "My last boyfriend and I had sex together (only a few weeks before meeting Mark), but it is not the same with Mark. We have sex because we love each other and we know that we will get married." The red flags immediately started waving in my mind. I ventured to ask Sharon about her parent's relationship, knowing the impact parents have on their children's behavior and on their relationships. "Oh, they got divorced when I was nine years old," she said. By then the red flags were flying with gale-force winds! I was very worried about Sharon's future!

I saw a young woman standing in front of me whose parents had a failed marriage. You have probably heard the saying, "more is caught than taught." After speaking with Sharon, I realized that the breakdown in her parent's relationship had added to her insecurity, and that she was ill prepared to make wise decisions regarding relationships. It was difficult for Sharon to know what to look for in a relationship when she had not seen it demonstrated at home. I saw her giving herself emotionally and physically to men, very soon after meeting them, with very little reservation. She was looking for love. She was desperate! And, the worst thing about it was, she was totally unaware of her dilemma! I was convinced that Sharon was ill-prepared to find love.

I tried in vain to help her understand that what she really needed was a relationship with God -to experience Him and His love, first and foremost. She did not need a man at this point in her life. She needed her Heavenly Father! Unfortunately, since she did not see there was a problem, there was nothing I could offer her at that time. That broke my heart on that beautiful fall day in South Carolina.

Well, as radio news commentator Paul Harvey always says, now you will hear "the rest of the story." Two weeks later, I returned to the USC campus and was again interacting with students at the same location. After an hour or so, Sharon saw me and came running up with a big smile on her face, proudly thrusting out her left hand for me to see her engagement ring. In her right hand she was dragging (you guessed it) Mark, her fiancй! She introduced me to Mark and we chatted for a while. I wished them the best in their future marriage. But, I had serious doubts about the success of their future together. I felt sick and saddened for Sharon and Mark, believing they were headed for a rocky marriage and possibly divorce in the next few years. What could I do to stop them? Nothing. After all, it's what they wanted. But, then I remembered there was something I could do. As I was walking to my car, I prayed and asked God to show Himself to Sharon and Mark. He made them and loved them dearly. Marriage was His idea. I know that God heard my prayer. (Maybe they will read this book some day!)

God knows what is best for His kids, for us. Let's discover the mystery of real security and contentment. Taking to heart the truths in this book can save you from an insecure life that can result in a miserable marriage, bitterness, major disappointment and possible divorce. Even if you are presently in an insecure relationship, there is hope for you! I promise!

Why do many of us go to parties, bars, church events, concerts, youth gatherings and other social events? Sometimes we are bored, empty, lonely and looking for someone to love us. If this is true, it's wise to be honest about our motives and to admit our weaknesses. We all have them, and the only way to become whole and healthy is to admit we have these deficiencies! That is why I went to Young Life Club in high school. There were a lot of attractive girls and everyone seemed to be having a great time! God was the farthest thing from my mind at the time. God used the people leading these youth events to draw me to Himself. It was there I first met real

> There is something missing in our life that is of far greater importance than a boyfriend, girlfriend or spouse.

Christians who showed me the source of life. And, the source of life was not the cute blond girl that I wanted to like me. What was the source of life?

We are all naturally lonely and searching for love, real friendships, and quality relationships. Is that the best reason to get married? No! If we are honest, it is why most of us pursue a serious relationship. We want to know somebody cares about us, that we are special to someone, and that they can't live without us. That is what I wanted! Am I saying it is wrong to want to be loved? Of course not! This is a legitimate need in the heart of every human on the planet. First we need to understand that there is something missing in our life that is of far greater importance than a boyfriend, girlfriend or spouse. There is something missing in each of our lives that must be satisfied, and it is foundational to a good marriage and to every healthy human relationship

God wants us to get married when we are secure in His love; content and complete. Only He can fill the void in our emotions. His love never changes. When we experience His all-satisfying love each day, it helps us operate in human relationships from strength instead of weakness. Although there is a lot of talk about love in our world, we seem to be ignorant about what love really is. Let's look into the mystery of God's love.

Discussion Questions
Chapter 1

1. In your opinion, why are so many couples unprepared for marriage?

2. Have you ever felt like you found the one, only to later realize you were mistaken?" Briefly describe your experience. What you were thinking at the time and why?

3. What are some potential "red flags" in any relationship?

4. How does Steve describe our natural state? This is the reason many people get married.

Chapter 2

Our family had just moved from Bethesda, Maryland to Atlanta, Georgia because my father had been transferred, again. He worked for thirty years for IBM (International Business Machines); also known to its employees as "I've Been Moved" because of how often they were transferred to other cities. My father was frequently out of town, teaching sales seminars or on sales calls, and away from the family he loved. This was the fifth city I had lived in and fifth set of new friends I had to make. I was a skinny little 8th grader who was overwhelmed with being in a new city, beginning North Springs High School as a sub-freshman. Yes, there were five grades in our high school and we were actually called sub-freshmen — the lowest on the food chain! I felt very lonely standing there on the high school sidewalk that first day of class in late August. I didn't know a soul. My father's frequent absences and all the changes in scenery had rocked my young world, making me even more insecure.

Therefore, I began my high school career, like many my age, highly motivated to find a group of friends where I could fit in. Who wants to be weird? I also began to feel the pressure to find a girlfriend and be "normal." I wanted her to care about me, and I wanted to know that I mattered to someone. But my insecurities held me back. I was shy and feared rejection more than being alone on a Friday night. To call a girl on the phone and ask for a date terrified me, because she might say no, and in fact,

---

I began to see women more and more as sex objects to satisfy my selfish desires, and not as real people with feelings, needs, and the right to be respected.

---

several did. This fear of rejection made pornography a natural solution. I could "be loved" by different women, lots of them, and never suffer rejection! It was safe. Or was it?

I did not have a clue that pornography would actually destroy my confidence and rob me of my manhood. It was so attractive, so beautiful and so easy! However, it only compounded the problem of how to relate to women in a healthy way. I began to see women more and more as sex objects to satisfy my selfish desires, and not as real people with feelings, needs, and the right to be respected. I was desperately looking for love from someone. My world was falling apart around me because I was becoming more and more selfish and self-centered. These verses from the Bible accurately described my life at the time. I was the "unloved man" looking for a wife.

*"Under three things the earth quakes, and under four, it cannot bear up: under a slave when he becomes king and a fool when he is satisfied with food, **under an unloved woman when she gets a husband,** maidservant when she supplants her mistress."*[1]

Earthquakes

God says that the "earth quakes" when certain things happen. Anyone who has been in a serious earthquake knows the destruction these powerful natural disasters can wreak. The rest of us have seen pictures or video of the awesome devastation that a major earthquake can bring. The more powerful earthquakes have twisted concrete and steel bridges like pretzels and leveled enormous high rise hotels and office buildings like children's toy blocks.

In the same way, there are earth-shaking problems when a slave becomes king. The slave is not experienced at leading others, or having this large amount of responsibility. He has always been told what to do, and usually with very limited responsibility. There would be serious problems in the kingdom if he were thrust into a position of leading the entire country with no preparation for the job.

Disaster strikes when a fool gets the food he has been craving. Why? What desire will the fool seek to satisfy next? Who will he hurt in the process? A fool is a person who makes poor choices without thinking through the consequences. These choices invariably hurt others as well as himself. The maidservant who takes over her mistress' position also precipitates numerous prob-lems. She demands her own way to the detriment of others, causing untold pain and suffering.

God never made a man to make a woman happy and He never made a woman to make a man happy.

What does it mean when the verse says that the earth quakes "under an unloved woman when she gets a husband?" What is wrong? Did her husband not love her? He may, or he may not have loved his bride. We don't know. He may have been a wonderful husband who truly cared about his wife and sacrificed his desires to meet her needs. That is not the issue. She entered the marriage relationship unloved and needy. Something was missing before she got married. Her expectations of her husband were impossible for him to fulfill. She was not experiencing God's supernatural love and therefore looked to her husband to meet her needs. He could not satisfy her needs, no matter how kind and compassionate a man he was. He was, and always will be, only a man. God never made a man to make a woman happy, and He never made a woman to make a man happy. Yes, men and women can bring a certain amount of joy into one another's lives. The relationship of a man and a woman in marriage is intended to bring deep satisfaction and joy.

But, we were never designed by our Creator to fulfill each other's deepest needs. This is our formidable problem, attempting to fulfill one another's deepest needs without the ability to do so!

The earth shakes every day in millions of marriages all over the planet. These earthquakes usually begin with minor tremors in the marriage, tremors of misunderstandings, hurt feelings, jealousy, unresolved conflict, neglect and boredom. Then they develop into the major quakes of verbal abuse, physical abuse, sexual addiction, drug addiction, adultery and divorce. What is the cause? The root of the problem is that we are not personally experiencing God's love (more on this latter) before we tie the knot, and therefore we enter the marriage relationship insecure and empty. We expect our partner to fulfill these deepest needs. When they cannot deliver, we may begin to look around for someone who can. Or we give up on finding love from a spouse, and turn to various hobbies and pleasures to try to make us happy. I believe that one of the greatest causes for drug and alcohol abuse is an unfulfilled relationship. How many stories have we heard, or movies have we watched, where the husband and/or wife turned to alcohol as a way to escape the emptiness of their marriage? Unsatisfied spouses also turn to material possessions, entertainment, fantasy novels, eating addictions, and virtual reality games to fill their emptiness and dull their pain. But, temporary escape from reality only makes reality harder to face. Trying to escape from our problems only makes them harder to deal with when we come back to them later on. Our problems do not go away, no matter how much we wish they would. Therefore, when we are sober again, or return from our vacation, or possess the new house or car, the problems are still there! Usually they have become worse. The "temporary escape" was only a temporary fix, like putting a band aid on Melanoma! Is there a cure that will help us face the danger of our reality — the reality of our unsatisfied need for love?

You were created to find fulfillment first and foremost through experiencing God and His amazing love. As the Psalmist said, *"Whom have I in heaven but you? I desire You more than anything on earth. My health may fail, and my spirit may grow weak, but God remains the strength of my heart; He is mine forever."*[2] While your mate may have significant issues, the root problem is within you! And no matter where you go, you can— not escape your own deficiencies. Wherever you go, YOU will be there! You must fix the problem within you.

Shattered American Dream

Bill and Jackie Ross appeared to most to have a happy marriage. Bill was outgoing, handsome, and had a great job. Everyone loved Bill, even the folks who worked for him! He had a way of making them feel important and would often roll up his sleeves and jump in and help them with their menial work, even though he was the boss. He and Jackie had just purchased a new home in the suburbs. Jackie stayed at home with their six and eight year old sons and enjoyed making pottery as a hobby. I still have one of her pieces on my dresser at home. They seemed to have what many would envy, a happy family, living the American dream. That is why their divorce was a shock to so many of their friends. My wife and I were closer to them than most, and we knew they were having difficulty in their relationship because they had asked for our counsel. We met together to help them understand each other and discover the cause of their frustrations. Many times we asked God to intervene on their behalf. We were still shocked when we heard about Jackie's bizarre actions that in the end led to the divorce. All the details came out during the heart-wrenching custody hearings. We heard about Jackie's infidelity during a preliminary hearing with Bill, Jackie, the judge, and their lawyers. Whereas her infidelity surprised us, her comments during the hearing stunned us. Here is what happened.

Bill's lawyer was asking Jackie some questions at this hearing. Bill's lawyer said, "Mrs. Ross, do you know Mr. Charlie Johnson?" (Charlie Johnson was the man with whom Jackie had had the affair.)
"Yes," she answered.
"Did you go to Hawaii with Mr. Johnson?"
Jackie replied, "Yes."
"Have you had sex with Mr. Johnson?"
Again she simply answered, "Yes."
"Do you love Mr. Johnson?"
She did not answer.
The lawyer repeated the question a little louder, as if she did not hear him,

"Do you love Mr. Johnson?"
She remained silent.
The lawyer, with some impatience in his voice, repeated a little louder,
"Mrs. Ross, do you **love** Mr. Johnson?"
With a look of confusion on her face she asked,
"What is love?"

I was shocked to hear about Jackie's response! How could someone give up a good marriage, loving family, and bright future for something she was not even sure existed? But isn't this true for many of us? We are unhappy with our present situation, feel unloved, and desperation drives us to do something foolish. Do you know what real love is? If you don't, what prevents you from doing something foolish like Jackie?

Bill was a fine young husband and father, but he was not equipped to satisfy Jackie's need for love, the love that only God could give her. Very simply, he was not God. He had his flaws and struggled with his own weaknesses and self-ishness as well. The sad reality was that Charlie, the new boyfriend, could not fulfill Jackie's need for love either! Remember, there is not a man on the earth who can meet a woman's need for love. And there is not a woman on the earth who can meet a man's need for love. Only God can!

I have lost track of Jackie. I am certain that one of three scenarios has played out. One, Jackie discovered that Charlie didn't have enough love either and lowered her expectations. Then she stopped searching and settled for a life of quiet desperation. Or two, she moved on to a third partner, seeking the mysterious concept of love. Or three, she found the love of her life in Jesus Christ! The fourth scenario gives one the foundation necessary to find their true partner.

People who have been divorced often get remarried, continuing their search for the perfect mate. They aren't out there! There are no perfect mates! There *is* someone who is "perfect for you" I believe. But, there is not a perfect person out there for you or anyone else! They don't exist. God is the only Perfect One and He alone can completely satisfy your need for love and security. And boy, can He!!!

Love Is More

Love, what is it anyway? Every day, all over the planet, we sing about love in our songs. Love is the main theme in thousands of our books and acted out in the majority of our movies. For all of our preoccupation with love, you would think that we would be experts by now! Every year there are millions of couples who get divorced. The number of cases of child abuse, spouse abuse, robberies, murders, and other crimes against humanity prove we do not love each other. As astronaut Jack Swigert, aboard Apollo 13 said, "Houston, we've had a problem." The number two oxygen tank had just exploded and the number one tank had also failed. The crew of the Apollo 13 was 200,000 miles above the earth at the time of the catastrophe. They had a very serious problem! Our problem is no less life-threatening.

Many marriages are destroyed because there is no real love. Love is much more than feelings for one another and similar goals and interests. These types of bonds are shallow and short-lived. The problem is that we don't know what love is, or we are too weak to love our spouse as we know we should, or both. How would you define love? Is love an emotion or physical attraction to someone? How can we love someone one minute, and then hurt them the next? How can we think the world of someone, and then find fault with them over insignificant issues? Is our love fickle? Do our ever-changing emotions provide the foundation to build a strong marriage? Are we too bewildered by the whole idea, as Jackie Ross was, when she profoundly said, "What is love?" Is it possible to have love in real life or is it merely a fantasy reserved only for couples in the movies?

> **How can we love someone one minute, and then hurt them the next?**

Love is more than an emotion or feeling. Feelings come and go. So do marriages that are built on the shifting sands of emotions and feelings!

Love is more than sharing common interests. Marriage is a relationship that involves our emotions, soul, and spirit. Sharing a similar love for tennis, Chinese food, Starbucks coffee, or the ocean only goes so far in bonding two lives together before you will run out of gas.

Love is more than a physical attraction. We marry a person — not just a body. No matter how hard we try to keep the ol' bod' in good shape through exercise, a healthy diet and proper rest; we just can't stop aging. A relationship that is primarily built on physical attraction is destined to fail from the beginning. Either we will be the spouse shopping for a newer model, or our insecurity will make us paranoid that someone younger and more attractive will come along and steal our spouse.

Love is more than compatible personalities. While it is important to have compatibility in marriage, it takes much more to weather the stress that every relationship faces. Compatible personalities will not bring us through when we hurt each other, or have to deal with our greed, lust, and fears. When others abuse us or take advantage of us, we need more strength from our marriage relationship to be able to forgive and love others.

Love is more than co-dependence. We were all created to need other people, but our greatest need for security can only be solved by the Greatest Person! There isn't another human who can satisfy that need. If we attempt to obtain our happiness from another person, we will only suck them dry. Then they will resent us for smothering them and want to escape. We were all created to live and breathe freely and independently of one another. We must also be dependent on one another for life. It seems like a paradox. It is vital that we be independent first! We must, "Get a life!" as the saying goes, before we can give to others. We will look at where you can "get a life" later in this book. This is a life with genuine love, the essential ingredient for a strong marriage.

Love is not something you simply fall into. Contrary to popular thinking, love is not something you fall into or out of, like tripping and falling into the river. Genuine love is a choice, and not something that happens to us that we cannot control. If it is only something we fall into, then falling out of it can be just as easy and fatalistic. Who wants a marriage built on such a weak foundation? "Falling in love" is dangerous grounds for a marriage, which implies the decision is totally out of our control and beyond reason.

> Love is a choice to sacrificially give to others, oftentimes when our feelings are telling us not to.

I love to run, and therefore I will go out in every kind of weather and run on every kind of terrain. Falling down is not something I enjoy doing, but it is inevitable for the fanatic runner like myself. One time in Kiev, I fell down the steps leading to the tunnel under the highway. My friend Timmy and I had just started our three mile run when I missed a step, rolled my ankle, and fell head-long down the stairs. Ouch! After getting over the initial shock and assessing my injury, I decided to continue our run. I felt al-

40

right during the rest of our time. But, the next day my ankle was purple and had swelled up like a giant sausage! I did not choose to fall; I was just carelessly taking two steps at a time. In the same way, "falling" in love is not a wise way to build a relationship. It can be dangerous and painful. Love is a choice to sacrificially give to others, oftentimes when our feelings are telling us not to. Love is never natural or easy, whereas falling is.

The Real Deal

God says that real love is self-sacrificial, patient, kind, and does not demand its own way. *"Love is patient and kind. Love is not jealous or boastful or proud or rude. It does not demand its own way. It is not irritable, and it keeps no record of being wronged. It does not rejoice about injustice but rejoices whenever the truth wins out. Love never gives up, never loses faith, is always hopeful, and endures through every circumstance."*[3]

This is the opposite of our human nature. We are naturally impatient and selfish people. When we don't get what we want, we often become angry, vengeful, or jealous. When someone hurts us, we want to get even and take revenge, either physically or verbally harming the other person. Sometimes, our pride and self-centeredness can even blind us to the point that we really don't care what is right or wrong.

God's definition of love is foreign to our cheap love, which is why many of our marriages crumble with just the slightest test. Having access to God's love is essential for a marriage that will weather the storms of life. We can be married and live under the same roof, but not be sacrificially committed to each other. The enthusiasm for one another's welfare has vanished, if it was ever there to begin with. We

When all that a couple does is share meals together, raise kids together, and sleep in the same bed; it is a far cry from God's plan for marriage.

may be physically together but emotionally divorced. When all that a couple does is share meals together, raise kids together, and sleep in the same bed; it is a far cry from God's plan for marriage where His love and joy are experienced by all.

One warm spring day in Clemson, South Carolina, I was having a discussion with a group of male students outside. At that time of the year, more than any other, the young men had women on their minds. Of course, some of the coeds did not help these guys with their thoughts by their provocative dress! A group of attractive coeds walked past our group and one of the guys blurted out, "I'm in love!" as he admired one coed's body. My spontaneous response was, "You're not in love, you're in lust! You don't even know her. How can you love someone you don't even know?"

This is exactly the way I used to think before I became a follower of Jesus Christ. I could relate to these young men and their natural, impulsive desires. I was extremely impatient, jealous of others, and often controlled by my lust and pride. I was totally in the dark when it came to understanding God's kind of love. If I was attracted to a woman, and had feelings for her, then I thought it must be love. Right? Wrong! Love *"does not seek its own,"* God tells us. Real love is much, much more than being physically attracted to someone. We are physically attracted to hundreds of the opposite sex in our lifetime, but it takes God's love to be truly committed to just one. Loyalty and devotion to one person requires God loving through us. It may seem impossible to love others in this way. Actually, it is! This caliber of love is against our nature. We do not have the natural capacity. But don't despair; here is how you can love others at a new level.

Discussion Questions

Chapter 2

1. Why is love so misunderstood?

2. We often equate love with sex. Why do they seem inseparable?

3. Steve describes his own battle with pornography. Why do you think it is so appealing?

4. How is real love contrasted with today's popular version of love?

5. Replace the word "love" with *your name* in the verses from 1 Corinthians 13. What does this exercise reveal about you?

QUICK AND EASY

Sveta is a single Ukrainian woman in her twenties. She has been a good friend of our family for many years, interpreting for us, and helping us to feel at home in another culture. I was involved in organizing and leading over thirty short term teams to Russia and Ukraine over a period of ten years. It was during one of these trips that I met Sveta and she became a follower of Jesus Christ. In 2005, my wife and I, along with our two youngest daughters, moved to Kiev to have a greater impact by living there. Until you have lived in someone else's world where they speak another language, have different thought processes, a different culture, and a different history -you cannot appreciate a Sveta who gives you confidence and helps you feel less foolish. Many times we have thanked God for His presence in the person of our friend Sveta. She told me recently how she had gone online searching for a potential husband. Her curiosity compelled her to discover what was out there in the world of available men and how internet dating would work. Her project was mainly based on curiosity. Who hasn't been curious? She simply wanted to see how the internet dating system worked. She told me how she communicated with several men, discussing common interests over a period of a few weeks. She was not desperate, not yet anyway. She was just "testing the waters" as we would say. Why would she do this? Why do thousands of single men and women use these services? Is

it just curiosity? Sometimes. Maybe they are bored? Often.
How frequently are they driven by desperate insecurity and
loneliness?

Old Maid

In Ukraine, you are considered an old maid if you reach
your mid-twenties and are not married. There is a tremendous amount of pressure from your parents and your
peers to find a husband before it is too late. This unnecessary pressure causes many women to become desperate
and lower their expectations. Therefore, they grab the
next available guy before they all get away. Many women
are willing to settle for a man of unproven character, or
even someone they know lacks integrity, because of their
fear of being alone. They will overlook character defects
in a po-tential mate in their desperation. This flawed
thinking may cause a woman (or man) to make fool-ish
decisions. She may be very attractive, but she lacks dis-
cernment about how to live wisely, *"Like a gold ring in
a pig's snout is a beautiful woman who shows no discretion."* [4] This is a dangerous place to be! An attractive
woman who acts foolishly looks like a pig with a beautiful gold ring in his nose. The contrast is **shocking!** She is
beautiful, but her behavior is in stark contrast to her appearance. Her poor judgment does not match her God-
given beauty, just like an expensive gold ring would look
very strange in the nose of a fat, dirty pig. Men and
women alike need to possess cautious discretion when
choosing a marriage partner!

The Comparison Trap

Another potential hazard when choosing a marriage partner is the quicksand of comparison. Lena asked me about Natalie, our mutual friend. When I told her that Natalie was expecting her third child, Lena asked, "How old is Natalie?" I told her and she said that they were the same age. She continued with discouragement in her voice, "It does not seem fair. Natalie is expecting her third child. I am the same age as Natalie, and there's no one in my life now who is even a potential husband!" I gently reminded her that God had not forgotten her, and that He loved her as much as He loved Natalie. I quoted God's promise to her, *"Since he did not spare even his own Son but gave him up for us all, won't he also give us everything else?"* [5] We discussed how having a husband and children did not automatically take away loneliness. Intellectually, she knew that God could be all she needed. Her emotions tempted her to doubt, but her heart told her told her that God was sufficient. He was more than enough for her needs. She began to see through the lie that hav-

She began to see through the lie that having a husband was essential to her happiness and that comparison is a trap.

ing a husband was essential to her happiness and that comparison is a trap. She was encouraged and thankful for God's goodness. God proved His love for Lena 2,000 years ago by Christ's death for her. She just needed to be reminded of this fact. This trap is one that Lena faces every day. We all face it, single and married alike. So, how are you doing today at avoiding the comparison trap? You must understand that your marital status really has nothing to do with your contentment or happiness. Lena left me that day with her faith renewed by the truth – free from the lies that cause desperation and often lead to foolish decisions. Jesus said, *"Then you will know the truth, and the truth will set you free."*[6] Believing God's truth will set you free from the lies you hear each day. Do you know the truth? Do you know the lies that have enslaved you through comparing yourself with others?

Find Your Soul Mate

"We will find a soul mate for you." This is the bold promise of a popular online dating service. What a promise! They will deliver my mail-order bride right to my doorstep! Wow! Of course I am exaggerating, but that's almost what that promise communicates to me. I get nervous when I hear the claim, "We will find a soul mate for you." I am sure there are single people who have used these services and are satisfied with the results. I have heard couples testify how the dating service worked for them, and how happy they are now with their new soul mate. I have no way of knowing exactly how effective these services are, but it seems dangerous to me. The end of the commercial says, "There are a lot of happy guys out there tonight." I think the greatest danger of this service is that it can encourage lonely singles to have "finding their mate" as the main goal of their life. If they just find that soul mate then they will be happy. Right? It isn't that simple.

Content Before Marriage

We need to discover what really brings joy and contentment before we find our spouse. I'm convinced that true happiness only comes from having a personal relationship with Jesus Christ, and not from finding the right mate. It is a perfectly normal human desire to want to be happily married. But, if I am not satisfied with life as a single person, then no one and nothing can make me happy. "Happiness" depends on our circumstances. If I get what I want, the way I want, and when I want, then I will be happy. If the circumstances do not go the way I want, then I become irritated, jealous, angry, or depressed.

On the other hand, joy comes from within — from experiencing Jesus Christ living in you, and not from your circumstances. Your circumstances may not be what you would choose, and yet you can still have joy, peace, and hope. God promises that His love for you will never change. *"He delights in unchanging love."*[7] Jesus demonstrated His love by dying for you on the cross. The issue of God's love for you was settled forever. No circumstance will ever change that. That fact is where your hope should rest. The worst thing that could ever happen to you will not separate you from Jesus Christ and His love. God's amazing, unchanging, unconditional love is yours once you come to know Jesus as your Savior and Lord. Now that is security! God and His love is the source of joy. Joy is also a by-product of knowing and living for God. It is not something you and I can manufacture. Joy is what God produces in you when you give Him control of your life. He will empower you to live for others and put their desires ahead of your own. When a husband chooses his wife's interests ahead of his own, then God's joy will be real to him. Most of us are seeking someone or something to make us happy. We have it backwards. Jesus said that we should deny our selfish desires and follow His example of love, *"Then he said to the crowd, 'If any of you wants to be my follower, you must turn from your selfish ways, take up your cross daily, and follow me.'"* [8] Our world encourages us be selfish and self-centered. We should take care of ourselves, first and foremost, because everyone else is. Jesus said that we will actually lose our life by selfishly holding on it, *"If you try to hang on to your life, you will lose it. But if you give up your life for my sake, you will save it."* [9] The wise decision is to agree with Jesus, who proved the validity of this principle through His own life. He had tremendous joy because He al-ways lived to please His Father and He always put the needs of others ahead of His own.

If you put God's interests and His purpose ahead of your own, then He will provide for all of your needs, including

---

✵

Our world encourages us be selfish and self-centered.

⚘

---

a spouse. Jesus said *"Seek the Kingdom of God above all else, and live righteously, and he will give you everything you need."* [10] "If you put God's interests and His purpose ahead of your own," — that is a huge variable! If you love God with all of your heart, soul, mind and strength, and your neighbor as yourself, then He will give you everything you need. If you need a mate, then God will bring you the specific person He intended for you to marry. He promises! Do you believe He can and will do that for you?

If you say, "Yes I do believe God's promise," this implies a lot about the object of your faith. It implies that you are convinced that God loves you with all of His heart and therefore you can trust Him completely. Do you know that the Father loves you as much as He does His own Son Jesus? Jesus prayed to His Father, *"May they experience such perfect unity that the world will know that you sent me and that you love them as much as you love me."* [11] When you are convinced of His amazing love for you it will have other positive ramifications. You will understand that God has all power and that He knows everything. You will become persuaded that He is in ultimate control of every circumstance — including every marriage. Including your marriage! If you are convinced that He loves you, and that He has the ability to provide for your needs, then you can focus on His purpose and other's needs. He will take care of providing your spouse. He promised, remember? I believe this is God's preferred way of bringing two people together as husband and wife.

Secure in Time

It took several years for me to get to the place where I was secure in God and would trust Him with this area of my life. It was a struggle! I know that it will be difficult for you too. For nineteen years I trusted my own ability to meet my needs. Choosing to give control to someone else was not nat-

I discovered that God's love for me never changed.

ural for me. Because I was a new Christian, and I could not see God, I often doubted His love for me. It took time before His love became a life-transforming reality. There were many ups and downs in our relationship. I was the one who was fickle, continuing to struggle with pornography, guilt, pride, and jealousy. The beautiful thing, I discovered, was that God's love for me never changed. He was equally committed to me when I failed or when I overcame these temptations. I started to understand that God only wanted my best and that obeying His commands would lead to my freedom and peace. He loved me unconditionally, and the more I tasted His love, the more convinced I became that He was trustworthy. He repeatedly proved Himself. Who do you know like that? Who is perfectly faithful, unchanging in his love, and will never leave you? Nobody on the planet fits this description! But we are all tempted to doubt God and His love. We are tempted every day to look at our circumstances and say, "If God really loved me, He would not allow *this* to happen to *me!*"

But God says He will not allow you to be tempted beyond what you can handle with His help. *"No temptation has overtaken you but such as is common to man; and God is faithful, who will not allow you to be tempted beyond what you are able, but with the temptation will provide the way of escape also, so that you will be able to endure it."*[12]

The way to escape the loneliness of being single comes from learning to enjoy Jesus and from serving others with God's strength. (You will find more on this subject in Chapter Seven) Then our kind Father in heaven will take care of any and every need you have, including your marriage partner. If you are growing in God's love and grace, and working for Him, it will give you an opportunity to associate with other singles who share a similar passion. These are the kind of people who are secure and whom God wants you to marry.

We have discovered how critical it is to experience God's love before we consider getting married. If we are separated from God and His life-giving love for us, then our insecurities will get the best of us. Our lives will often be characterized by jealousy, loneliness, impatience, and general selfishness, which will control us and potentially destroy every relationship. There is no quick and easy way to find your soul mate. Impatience is a manifestation of selfishness and insecurity and leads many singles in a vain attempt to find their soul mate. God is often not a part of the equation, even though He longs to be. He will call to us in a soft voice and it's up to us to respond — to ask for His help and trust His love and wisdom.

I visited the web site for the city of Chernigov, Ukraine to find out the city's population. The first thing that caught my attention, especially since I was writing this book, was the advertisement under "Marriage Agency." It was created for single women who were looking for a husband. I clicked on the blinking photo of the woman. This opened the site to more pictures, names and details of over 1100 women of various ages, appearances and occupations! It was interesting to read what these women were looking for in a husband — honest, loyal, caring, faithful, kind, and loves children. They had high expectations. Here is one from Elena, "I seek an attentive, kind, polite, joyful, sincere man who loves children and who is pleasant to speak to." How many of these women found the husband of their dreams? Or how many were willing to compromise, because of their insecurities, and were willing to settle for a man who would help them escape from Ukraine to a "better life" in Europe or North America?

"You don't have to be rich, handsome, famous or lucky to have a beautiful, devoted wife. Simply start corresponding with the women of Kiev Connections and take the first step to realizing the dream life of every man." This is the byline from a marriage agency in Kiev. What are most men attracted to first? Honestly, for most men, the first question we have is — What does she look like? We want to know if she is pretty, her age, her size, and the color of her hair. God created men to be attracted to women, but that does not mean it is the wisest way to find a wife. God tells us what really matters is a person's heart, *"for God sees not as man sees, for man looks at the outward appearance, but the Lord looks at the heart."*[13] The women in Kiev Connections are emphasizing their looks, putting their best face out there, because they too know what men are drawn to. Women will go to all lengths to look great for the camera, when this is not the most important quality they possess. You have to wonder, why do they say they want a husband who is honest, loyal, caring, faithful, kind, and loves children; and then go to such great lengths to promote their appearance? If a relationship is built on the shifting sands of appearance, it is destined to fail. Sadly, many are, and many do. I am sure this isn't what you want, or you would not be reading this book.

Desperate and Vulnerable

Desperation makes you vulnerable to pain and hardship. If you are insecure, you will "sell your soul" to the highest bidder. You will go to all lengths to find someone who will have you, even if it means you have to compromise. "He is an honest person. I know he can be unkind some times, but he has a good job and will take care of me. Besides, I know that I can change him." Compromising our values and morals causes us to sell ourselves cheaply, and reveals that we don't think we are worth very much.

It reminds me of the American television show *Desperate Housewives*. As the title implies, these women compromise their morals every week because their insecurities make them desperate. I would imagine that the men on the show are equally desperate and immoral. The more desperate we are, the more likely we are to give our heart and soul to someone who shows the least bit of interest in us. That is why it is important to come to know Jesus Christ as your Savior, as your primary hope. Only then can you begin to experience His love and see how valuable you really are. The more you experience His love, the higher your standard becomes and the "price of your stock" goes up. You realize that you are of great worth to God. Your "selling price" to a potential marriage partner increases when your insecurities decrease.

You will not sell out at the first offer of marriage because you are afraid there will not be any others. You will look deeper than the outward appearance, beyond simply the words and promises of love, past the false security of money and social status to the real person. You will examine their character over a period of time, especially in difficult situations.

Will you settle for going through the drive-thru and ordering a fast food relationship?

You will wait patiently for the person God wants to give you, and not be desperate. You will think and not just feel. You will seek the counsel of mature friends, and not do anything rash.

You will be strong enough in Jesus' love that you can say "no" without regrets to the offers from those who pursue you who lack character and genuine sacrificial love.

Finding the right spouse will never be quick and easy. Most of the things in life that advertise themselves as quick and easy end in disaster! We are lured by quick and easy sex, quick money, quick success, quick weight loss, and fast food. They can be dangerous lies that many of us have fallen for. Do you agree with God, when He says that anything in life worth having takes effort? *For the dream comes through much effort!*[14] Are you willing to make the effort to realize the dream God has for you? Or will you settle for going through the drive-thru and ordering a fast food relationship? Will your insecurities cause you to get what you want now, or postpone your immediate desires for a genuine, soul-nourishing marriage? The follow-ing is a true story about how insecurity drove someone to seriously consider a bizarre action to obtain what they wanted.

"Sex would be boring if you only had one partner!" Isaac insisted as we debated what made a healthy marriage. Isaac was a Jewish graduate student I met in front of the University of Georgia Student Union. We developed a mutual respect and appreciation for one another that grew out of the many discussions we had. Today we were discussing what constituted a strong, happy marriage. I said, "Isaac, I think boredom is often the result of being selfish. A variety of sexual experiences with other women will not take away your boredom. If you have a good relationship with your spouse, I guarantee that you will not be bored and you will have a great sex life!" I was curious what his wife would think of his bizarre comments. Yes, Isaac was married! So I asked him what she thought about his reasoning and he said, "She wants me to have sex with other women because we can't have children." Wow! "Have you all considered adoption instead?" I asked. He said that his wife was perfectly fine with him having sex with other women if they could conceive and have a child. She sounded like another desperate housewife!

They prescribe their relational medicines and perform their marital operations, but most of the time their diagnosis is flawed.

Have you ever wondered why God says we should have only one husband and one wife and not numerous partners? Does He want to spoil our fun? Never! Actually, God is the only one who knows what real, wholesome fun is! He knows that a marriage will not survive without trust, loyalty, and selfless devotion. Sex outside of marriage by any other name, is still adultery and destructive! I have never met a truly satisfied adulterer. Isaac would destroy his fragile marriage if he had sex with someone other than his wife. I sincerely wanted him to come to Yeshua, the Messiah, so that he could experience the forgiveness of his sins, and have the ability to love his wife, as never before. God was seeking Isaac! But, like so many students, he was not convinced that he had a problem.

Nobody goes to the doctor when they are healthy. We go when we feel bad, our head hurts or we have a fever. We know something is wrong, even if we are not sure what it is. That's when we call the doctor. In order for us to know how to get well we must have a correct diagnosis of our illness or disease. If we never have an accurate diagnosis of the problem, it won't matter how many different medications we take or operations we endure. The medicine would be a waste of time. The medicine must match the illness if it is to cure us. Often, we don't have a clue what is wrong with us. We hear the authorities make bold and convincing diagnoses of our relational problems, but many times they are quacks! They are merely offering their best educated guesses. We are convinced they should be trusted because they have college degrees, have written books, have a successful television show, and speak with authority. But, we fail to look deeper at their diagnosis of our marriage failures. They prescribe their relational medicines and perform their marital operations, but most of the time their diagnosis is flawed. We are guilty of not looking carefully at the results of their advice. Are the marriages they "operate on" healthier, and more secure with stronger commitment and respect? Now we will diagnosis your relational illness. Notice that I said "we." That is because you must tell me where it hurts and together we must try to understand why it hurts.

How did you get where you are today? Don't worry; I am speaking as "one beggar telling another beggar where to find bread." In other words, I too needed help, and still do! I needed the true Physician to diagnosis my illness and prescribe his cure. He is amazing! Here is how God referred to the true Physician, Jesus Christ, *"I am laying in Zion a chosen (honored), precious chief Cornerstone, and he who believes in Him [who adheres to, trusts in, and relies on Him] shall never be disappointed or put to shame."* [15] The Physician is ready to prove to you that He can be trusted!

Discussion Questions
Chapter 3

1. What makes us think that finding a marriage partner could be quick and easy?

2. When we want something "quick and easy" what does this usually reveal?

3. What effect has "the comparison trap" had on you in the past?

4. Isaac thought that having sex *only* with his wife would be boring. What do you think of his logic?

How Did I Get This Way?

Imagine you are standing on a stool which is on top of an 18 story building. You are on the outside edge looking down at all the ant-size cars and people down below. You are not worried though, because you have a good sense of balance and the stool has four steady legs. Well, you are not *too* worried. But what if the stool only had three legs? Would you feel as confident or as secure? How do you think you would feel if it only had two legs? If the stool only had one leg, you would immediately leap to safety on the flat roof, unless you were one of those circus performers who live for the thrill of facing death in front of a large crowd!

We all live on a stool, so to speak. Everyone's stool has a different number of legs and the number can change each day. Your circumstances determine how many legs you have on your stool. For example, what kind of love did you receive at home? Did your mother and father hug you, listen to you and praise you? Did they affirm you and build your confidence? Or, perhaps your mother or father was an alcoholic. Then one of the legs on your stool was removed. Are your parents divorced? Another leg was taken away. Were you ever abused? Each of these actions has a positive or negative effect on your security -how many legs your stool has to support you. Every missing leg, every deficiency, affects your ability to make wise decisions, and clouds your ability to choose your marriage partner. It is also necessary to understand that even with the most loving and positive family environment, we must not expect that this alone will guarantee us security and contentment. These factors influence us positively or negatively, but none of these are the main issue.

Like Father Like Son

Don was a legend in his own mind. I am sure you know someone like Don. He was the young man who built our house in the suburbs of Atlanta. He could do many things well, but the problem was, he thought he was an expert in everything! He was afflicted with what I call the "One-Up disease". Whatever you had accomplished, and were proud of, Don had done the same thing, only better! If you told him about the time you caught a large bass, he would immediately respond with his own story about the larger fish he caught. If you had installed a tile floor in your tiny bathroom one Saturday, he insisted that he had installed a tile floor in his entire eat-in kitchen in only four hours! I wondered to myself, why did Don insist on bragging? He alleged that he had done everything others had, only faster, bigger and better! My conclusion -it was his pride. His pride was the result of his deep insecurity! It was his defense mechanism that protected his fragile self-image. In fact, he was hurting inside.

Don's parents were divorced and so was he. Divorce can create powerful insecurities in children. Don told me of a time when he was having sex with his girlfriend at home, and his dad walked in on them, and never said anything. His dad's leniency was destructive and helped to create a son who was confused about right and wrong. There was no shame in Don's voice when he told me the story of his father finding him in bed with his girlfriend. He had been given no moral compass. Leniency that permits blatant immorality is unloving. Therefore, Don was still looking for love, and the best way he knew how was to "one up" everyone he met. He never listened very well because he was

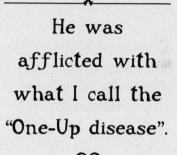

He was afflicted with what I call the "One-Up disease".

always thinking ahead to one of his own achievements to provide evidence of his worth. He zealously competed in sports and bass fishing contests to prove his manhood. If he could win on the ball field, or in a fishing contest on the lake, it made him feel better about himself. But Don remained bound by his deep insecurities, resulting in a socially deficient and obnoxious person. No wonder his marriage failed. Who could live with someone like that? It broke my heart to see Don blinded to his own weaknesses. His pride would not allow anyone else in to share his pain and loneliness.

Do you know where your insecurities originated? All of us may be more like Don than we want to admit. Admitting there is a problem is the first step to a solution. How did you become the person you are today? What kind of relationship did your parents have? Are they divorced? Are they married, but just living together? Some couples endure each other for the sake of their children. Don't you think the children sense something is missing? Of course they do! Your parents' relationship greatly influences your security. But don't despair; there is hope for all of us!

One day I was working on this book in a restaurant near our apartment in Kiev. I mentioned to the waitress that I was writing about how to have a good marriage, because so many marriages fail in America and Ukraine. With a sudden serious look on her face, she responded in a sober tone of voice, "My parents are divorced too." She went on to tell me how happy she was that I was writing this book. "My purpose is to help the people of Ukraine have great marriages," I reassured her. First we must understand what we are doing wrong in our marriage. We have seen that it is essential to have an accurate diagnosis of the problem before a remedy is prescribed.

All In The Same Boat

All mankind is insecure! Can such a broad-sweeping statement be made? I think the evidence is obvious that every person who has ever lived was born with insecurities. The insecurities of some are so blatant that we are in awe of the horror and evil perpetrated on mankind by these madmen. What provoked Joseph Stalin to have millions of people murdered during his dictatorship? The estimates are between 10 and 20 million died as a result of deportation, execution, and famine. Whenever Stalin felt threatened by an individual, or a group of people, he acted with unrestrained violence to destroy his opposition. In his early years, Stalin feared political rival Serge Kirov, considering him a dangerous competitor for ruling in the Soviet Union. It is widely believed that Stalin had him assassinated. Feeling threatened, Stalin deported numerous ethic groups and intelligentsia. An estimated 3.3 million were sent to Siberia, where hundreds of thousands died en route or in concentration camps. Stalin had his comrades killed because of his suspicions, but had no valid reason to do so — now *that* was insecurity! We see another example of how insecurity is inseparably tied to pride. Stalin was one of the most arrogant men who ever lived, proudly accepting the following titles — "Father of Nations," "Brilliant Genius of Humanity," "Great Architect of Communism," and "Gardener of Human Happiness." Do you think the millions of innocent victims he had killed would agree with these absurd claims? The truth is — Stalin was a terrorist.

Stalin was an extreme example of insecurity and pride. While the average person is not so violently evil, we still have our own haunting insecurities. Some of us get angry and call people names, or do unkind things to others when they don't agree with us. We may act like Don the builder, to some degree or other. If we can't get what we want, and we don't see any way of changing the situation, we may force our way on others or manipulate them. Our insecurity is a consequence of being separated from God. We chose to turn from God (the Bible calls this sin) which resulted in our separation from Him and His love. This is why

When the first man and his wife (Adam and Eve) turned their backs on God, they exchanged real security for false security.

we are enslaved to our passions, lusts, fears, and selfishness. When the first man and his wife (Adam and Eve) turned their backs on God, they exchanged real security for false security. Their pride — thinking they could be wiser than their Creator — was their downfall. Sadly, it's ours too.

Everyone else in the world is enslaved and insecure like you. This is a universal problem! This fact can motivate you to understand your own weaknesses and explain why you act as you do. We are all in the same boat — starving for love! Usually, we are looking in all the wrong places -everywhere but up, up to God.

We can see insecurity revealed in every aspect of the human experience. Wherever you have insecure humans you will have:

- Insecure marriages
- Insecure families
- Insecure friendships
- Insecure businesses
- Insecure governments
- Insecure churches
- Insecure organizations
- Insecure teams

These are all led by insecure people, leaders who are motivated by weakness, fear, doubt and selfish ambition. Insecure leaders want to look good in the eyes of their followers and place too much emphasis on public opinion. Let's look closely at one famous leader.

An Insecure King

Saul was a man who had it all, a natural born leader! He was one of the most handsome men in Israel and considerably taller than his fellow Israelites. Saul would be a prime choice for an NFL quarterback or politician today. However, having natural abilities cannot remove one's insecurity, and it certainly didn't in Saul's case. He was afraid of people more than he respected God. When Saul was caught in a lie, he admitted his fear of people, *"I have sinned; I have indeed transgressed the command of the Lord and your words, because I feared the people and listened to their voice."* [16] He disobeyed God's clear command because he worried about how the people would react if they did not get what they wanted. Why did he cave in to popular opinion? He was deeply insecure! Saul's pride eventually cost him the kingdom, his own life, and even the life of his loyal son Jonathan.

Fear makes us stupid! It can take an intelligent adult and turn them into a child. It did with King Saul. He was a naturally competent man who was given the charge of leading an entire nation. Saul had the same natural weaknesses that have beset all mankind. He craved respect, honor and popularity so much that he violated his own conscience. He compromised; doing only part of what had God told him to do. Therefore, God removed the kingdom from Saul because of his disobedience. What caused King Saul to sacrifice his integrity and his relationship with God? What was worth risking the honor and power of the kingdom? Sadly, he valued the loyalty of his followers more than his loyalty to God.

False security can come in the form of our appearance, our accomplishments, or our possessions. While there is certainly nothing wrong with looking good or being successful, these will never completely fulfill us. Placing our hope in these can be deceptive and lead to false security. They can temporarily make us feel good about ourselves, but they can never deliver real and lasting security.

Uncontrolled Fears

Glenn's company recently finished building a beautiful new dam in North Georgia. Glenn and his wife Joy are good friends of ours from our days spent together in Clemson,

South Carolina. They took my wife and I to see this amazing project shortly before it was completed. We were spellbound as we stood near the massive concrete dam and gazed out over hundreds of acres of tree-covered land and imagined the entire area covered with water someday. The lake has the potential to provide drinking water and recreation for thousands of Atlanta residents. But, because the dam was not working yet, the area was dry and worthless. The river had to be controlled for the lake to be filled up and useful.

If you have uncontrolled fears, you are deficient in God's love and unable to reach your potential. The fear of being alone and unloved can cripple you! You are like a dam that was never put to use. It has great potential, but the lake bed remains dry and empty until the water is controlled. In the same way, our fears can leave us feeling dry and empty. God and His love may seem distant or imaginary — like a fairy tale. How can your free-flowing fears be controlled so that you will fulfill your purpose on earth?

Only God's love has the power to control your fears! What is the opposite of love? While hatred is a correct response, the Bible also tells us that the opposite of love is fear. "Perfect love expels all fear."[16] If you truly believe that God loves you, and only has your best in mind, then His love will expel all of

Only God's love has the power to control your fears!

your fears. His love closes the dam; it controls every anxious thought and will give you peace. His love, when you truly experience it, believe it, and rest in it, will overpower your worries and doubts. That may sound impossible when you first hear it, but God is the God of the impossible. He can do things you will never be able to do. God still works miracles today, *"He who...works miracles among you."* [17] Do you need a miracle in your relationships? God is ready and willing to give you one! He is simply waiting on *you* to ask in faith.

If your best friends are insecure and anxious about finding their mate, it will rub off on you.

What are you afraid of? Are you afraid of being single for the rest of your life? I remember how those thoughts used to upset me when I was single. The fear of being rejected and alone can drive us to do foolish things. We all remember Y2K and the rampant fears that spread like a wildfire. We were afraid the computers would crash, the phone systems would fail, and we would all be without water, electricity, and food for months. My wife and I had more than one conversation about what food and supplies to stockpile before January 1, 2000. We were all relieved when nothing happened after all. But, at the time, our fears were real and seemed to feed on each other. Every time I spoke to someone who was worried about what hardships Y2K could bring, I would leave them with my own fears multiplying. Fear feeds fear! We all look back now and laugh as we remember what precautions we took to avoid the imminent danger. The catastrophe never happened. Our fears, it turned out, were unfounded.

If you associate closely with others who are controlled by their fears, they will feed yours. If your best friends are insecure and anxious about finding their mate, it will rub off on you, resulting in your own anxiety growing instead of shrinking. Keep them as your friends, but develop friendships with wise men and women who can become strong, positive influences in your life. God says that close association with wise people is to our benefit, *"Become wise by walking with the wise; hang out with fools and watch your life fall to pieces."*[19] Choose to be influenced by men and women of faith. People who trust in God's ability to care for them, and to provide their mate, will be people of peace. They can help you to rest in God's goodness too.

Your fear can make you desperate to the point that you foolishly marry someone, only to regret your decision later on after the "I dos" are exchanged and life happens. Maybe you have begun to understand that the person beside you in bed is not able to drive out your fears and give you happiness. I hope so. It is my conviction that only the security derived from God's love will transform you from a fearful person to one of peace and contentment. Here God promises His perfect peace will be yours if you trust Him, *"You will keep in perfect peace all who trust in you, all whose thoughts are fixed on you!*"[20] God wants you to trust Him with your entire life, including your future or present mate. He promises you His perfect peace if you choose to trust Him.

False Security

We naturally place our confidence in many things to give us security, all of which will fail us at some point. Here God warns us about placing our hope in wealth. *"When you set your eyes on it, it is gone. For wealth certainly makes itself wings like an eagle that flies toward the heavens."*[21] Our finances can be lost overnight. Our physical appearance will change. Our new clothes will wear out and fashions change. The beautiful new car may rust, be stolen, or be in a wreck. Even your mind and body will slow down as you age. Is there anything that cannot be taken away from us? Is there a place to find true security that is unchanging? Yes! Only in the person of Jesus Christ can you and I find real and lasting security, eternal security. First we must see through all the false securities the world offers us before we will choose to trust in Christ alone. Now we will delve into the elusive, but critical, state of contentment.

Discussion Questions
Chapter 4

1. How have you lost legs on your stool?

2. In what ways are you like your mother and/or father?

3. Why is it so difficult for us to admit our insecurities?

4. Steve writes about the impact our friends have on our security. What effect are your friends having on your relationships?

5. Can you honestly verbalize (or communicate) your fears?

Chapter 5

Is Contentment Possible?

Man or Mouse

There was a student in my high school that always got into fights. He incessantly talked tough, acted cool and started fights with other students. Your first image of this student would probably be of some well-built athlete who could beat the fool out of anyone and was known as the school bully. Biff was just such a bully. Biff was Marty's (actor Michael J. Fox) nemesis in the movie *Back to the Future*. He was a large, dumb, obnoxious student who instilled fear in the hearts of all who opposed him. It was just the opposite at my high school. The young man with the short fuse who started all the fights was called "Mouse" because he was such a little fellow. Why did we continually hear stories about Mouse getting into another fight? By the way, Mouse usually won these fights, even against guys much bigger than he. It is my opinion that He was trying to overcome his feelings of insecurity about his size by proving his manhood in hand-to-hand combat. He was a fierce competitor with a short fuse. Unfortunately, I know this from personal experience. One day in Phys Ed class I was chosen to be his wrestling partner. Mouse exploded and quickly won the match. (Of course, this did not help my low self-esteem, to lose in front of my peers to someone half my size!)

You may not be a little man, but you may still view yourself as mouse-like. You may be 6'4" and weigh 255 pounds and be the starting linebacker on your college football team, but act like you have to constantly prove your manhood. You may feel pressure to prove, "I have what it takes," "I am strong," and "I'm a real man." Is this how real men act? Does a real man need to constantly prove himself? No! A real man is a secure man. Real confidence does not emanate from mortal combat on a football field, or from winning a fight in the parking lot after school

> I think before we have true confidence we must experience contentment.

Real manhood is not the result of "conquering" women in bed (or in your imagination). It doesn't depend on the amount of money you make, being the top salesman, or what kind of car you drive. What is a real man? Where should you discover your security and manhood? Are you a man or a mouse? I was a mouse. I was ignorant about true manhood and the peace and freedom that follow. I am truly thankful to God that He graciously revealed this principle to me.

I think before we have true confidence we must experience contentment. It is essential for a man to be content with who he is if he expects to have godly confidence. Our confidence cannot be tied to our performance or our possessions. A man must be at peace with himself, and that comes from being at peace with God. God says *"Only in returning to Me and resting in Me will you be saved. In quietness and confidence is your strength."*[22] True strength, for men and women, is received from God and produces an inner quietness and confidence. Genuine, godly confidence springs from contentment. A woman's confidence can't be tied solely to her appearance, her work, or her children. Let's examine this mysterious state so that we may be prepared to create our own deeply satisfying marriage. Can we become men and women who are content before we get married? I think we must!

Contentment

"Not that I speak from want,
for I have learned to be content
in whatever circumstances I am."[23]
(Paul writing from jail)

Contentment seems to be an elusive state of being for most of us. Many of you reading this book may not believe it is even possible to live in such a state of being. What is contentment? It is not simply settling for less, becoming a monk, and living in a state of self-denial. It isn't living without ambition or a desire to improve your life. Contentment is not avoiding conflict or difficulties. It is a choice to find joy and peace through a relationship with Jesus Christ. Contentment is something we must learn, because it is obviously missing when we are born into this world. Our rebellion against God, and consequent separation from Him and His love, makes all of us a bunch of malcontents! We will continue in this state of discontentment until this separation from God is repaired. Our personal discontent leaches into our marriage, and every other relationship, like toxic chemicals into a city's clean drinking water.

Contentment shouldn't be dependent upon our circumstances, our accomplishments or what we own. All of these can elicit strong emotions, which often rise and fall, depending on how we think life is treating us. We can go from feeling elated one minute, to feeling depressed the next, contingent upon the circumstances. This is shaky ground to build a marriage, or a life, upon! If our joy stems from our circumstances, we will constantly be riding an emotional

When our faith is totally in God, our circumstances don't control us, we live above them!

roller coaster. I think most of us would define happiness as the feeling of pleasure and delight that comes when things are going our way. If we get *what* we want, *when* we want it, and *how* we want it — then we are happy. A beautiful spring day, receiving a significant raise at work, a first date with that special person, great results on a chemistry exam, or your teenager cleaning his room without complaining, are events that make us happy! Good feelings follow positive circumstances. Who doesn't feel good when traffic is unexpectedly light and your typical hour commute to work only takes thirty minutes? Bad circumstances, such as failing an exam, breaking off your engagement, or getting a large, unexpected bill, can make us feel sad, angry, lonely or depressed. Therefore, circumstances can toss us up and down like a wave on the sea. But, when our faith is totally in God, our circumstances don't control us as we learn to live above them! We choose to trust God, His word, and His unchanging love, and choose not to hope in our ever-changing environment.

Aubrey Montague, one of the characters in <u>Chariots of Fire</u>, possessed this mysterious contentment. <u>Chariots of Fire</u> is a true story written by W. J. Weatherby and became an Oscar winning movie. Aubrey was one of the exceptional young student athletes from Cambridge University who competed in the 1924 Olympic Games in Paris, France. His friend, and fellow Olympic athlete, Harold Abrahams, could not understand such contentment. Abrahams, who was Jewish, had trained long and hard to make it to the Olympic Games, only to have lost his pre-vious race. He came in second to the American, Charlie Paddock, in the 400 meters. He had overcome numerous obstacles, not the least of which was living as a Jew in a Protestant country, to have this opportunity to prove to the world what he could do. He was facing his final race, the 100 meters, and fighting his doubts and feeling intense internal pressure. It was his last chance to win a gold medal and demonstrate that he was the fastest man in the world. Harold made this profound statement to his friend Aubrey, while his trainer, Sam Mussabini, was giving him a massage in the hotel room. "You, Aubrey, are my most complete man." He went on to expound, "You're

---

That's your secret – contentment. I'm twenty-four and I've never known it. I'm forever in pursuit and I don't even know what it is I'm chasing.

---

kind, compassionate, brave. A contented man. That's your secret — contentment. I'm twenty-four and I've never known it. I'm forever in pursuit and I don't even know what it is I'm chasing."[24] Abrahams' comment about not knowing what he was chasing sounds a lot like our friend Jackie from the first chapter when she asked, "What is love?" She too was not sure what she was chasing.

Both Abrahams and Jackie knew that there was something missing in their lives, but they really weren't sure what it was! Abrahams went on to say that his reason for living came down to his performance in the 100 meters. "And now in one hour's time, I'll be out there again. I'll raise my eyes and look down that corridor four feet wide with ten lonely seconds to justify my whole existence."[25] Do you ever feel like that, having to justify your existence? What self-inflicted pressure are you under to prove that you should exist? That is a terrible way to exist, and that's all it is — existing! It is certainly not living — living free and content! How can you become a content person like Aubrey Montague? Should we compete, as Abrahams did, to get what we want in life, in marriage? To know the answer to this question, we must look into competition and its effect on our lives.

Competition

Aubrey realized that his good friend Harold was obsessed with beating the renowned Scottish runner, Eric Liddell, to the point that he neglected his academics and friendships. "Watching Harold practicing an even faster start, Aubrey suspected that the Scottish runner now represented all that Harold felt he was competing against in the world. The fair-haired, modest Liddell, so secure in his Christian beliefs and so spontaneous in his running, was certainly the opposite of Harold, the dark, defensive competitor, driven by a need to prove himself continually."[26] Eric Liddell was secure in God's love for him, producing in him peace and confidence of a different variety than Abrahams'. What type of confidence do you possess? What drives you?

We can all be unwavering when it comes to getting what we want in life. That is not wrong by itself. There is such a thing as good, healthy competition. There is also such a thing as unhealthy competition that harms others and backfires on us. Unhealthy ambition leads to destructive competition. God describes it in this way, *"For where you have envy and selfish ambition, there you find disorder and every evil practice."*[27] This person is motivated by selfishness, greed or some other impure motive. God calls this self-centered attitude sin. He warns us that selfish ambition will result in disorder and every evil practice. Selfish ambition and unhealthy competition is no way to find a mate! We must first become free of our selfishness and insecurity and become complete men and women before we look for our marriage partner.

On the other hand, healthy ambition results in healthy competition, competition that is positive and builds others. *"Therefore we also have as our ambition, whether at home or absent, to be pleasing to Him."*[28] We see that healthy ambition seeks to please God, build up others, and not to please ourselves. *"So then we pursue the things which make for peace and the building up of one another."*[29]

Some of us have gone to great lengths and taken extreme measures to get that particular boyfriend or girlfriend. We have been competitive because we believed that we needed that person to complete our life. Sometimes these measures have hurt others, even our family and close friends. I know there were times in my life when I acted this way. Take a few minutes to honestly reflect on the actions and motives in your past and present relationships.

This kind of unhealthy competition reveals our deep insecurity, which does not pass away with age. It must be tackled as soon as possible. Insecurity breeds an unhealthy competitive spirit. When people are secure in God and His love, they are relaxed and at peace, because they know that God will take care of them. He will supply everything they need, including their husband or wife! *"That is what the Scriptures mean when they say, "No eye has seen, no ear has heard, and no mind has imagined what God has prepared for those who love him."*[30] Therefore, the question you must answer is, do you believe this? Do you believe that God cares that much about you personally and is powerful enough for you to trust Him completely?

It is the insecure who are always anxiously forcing their own way in life, often without realizing it. They may push, threaten, manipulate, or control others in order to get their

---

Do you believe that God cares that much about you personally and is powerful enough for you to trust Him completely?

own way. Sometimes, even when they obtain their goal, conquer their foes, and obtain the "prize," they are unsatisfied and long for more. *"Human desire is never satisfied."*[31] Contentment escapes the insecure. They may get the "guy of their dreams" and then wonder what happened. "I thought he would make me happy!" Or, the man snags the girl he has been fighting off others to have, and he begins to have second thoughts. "I thought she would make me look good and feel like a real man." Something is missing! The nagging doubts kill the insecure person.

The Secret

The Apostle Paul said that contentment was a secret he had to learn through living — facing hardship as well as pleasure. You may respond, "If I had a million dollars, I know I would be content!" Actually, you wouldn't, because money does not bring contentment. If it did, the rich would be the happiest people on earth. If we honestly ponder the issue, it becomes obvious, wealth does not produce joy, *"A glad heart makes a happy face; a broken heart crushes the spirit."* [32] The next time you see a *candid* photo of a wealthy person, notice if they are smiling. Why do the rich and famous often jump from spouse to spouse and from house to house? They too are searching for the elusive secret of contentment. Someone once asked a billionaire the following question about money, "How much is enough?" He answered, "Just a little bit more." How much is enough for you?

Contentment is not learned through hearing the lecture, "Find Contentment through Meditation." Contentment is learned through the school of difficulty, hardship and responsibility. It was a truth Paul had internalized. He chose to be content over and over, day after day, in every cir-cumstance he faced. Here are his words, *"Not that I speak from want, for I have learned to be content in whatever circumstances I am. I know how to get along with humble means, and I also know how to live in prosperity; in any and every circumstance I have learned the secret of being filled and going hungry, both of having abundance and suffering need. I can do all things through Him who strengthens me.*"[33]

Free In Prison

What can we learn about contentment from this seasoned apostle? By the way, are you aware of the circumstances surrounding Paul's writing of this letter to the Philippians? He is not reporting from his air-conditioned suite at the Rome Hilton. He is writing from Rome's Central Prison, and he is the prisoner!

*"Now I want you to know, brethren, that my circumstances have turned out for the greater progress of the gospel, so that my **imprisonment** in the cause of Christ has become well known throughout the whole praetorian guard and to everyone else, and that most of the brethren, trusting in the Lord because of my imprisonment, have far more courage to speak the word of God without fear.*"[34]

These ominous circumstances make what Paul has to say much weightier. We listen to anyone who has been through persecution, and hasn't quit on the human race or God. Paul has not soured and become hateful because of the unwarranted abuse. Paul was innocent of all charges against him. He was facing the death sentence, and yet he was still cheerful! How? He chose not be destroyed by bitterness, as we can see from his own words, *"Rejoice in the Lord always; again I will say, rejoice!"* [35] We respect the POW who did not succumb to bitterness, but instead — grew stronger, with more resolve and greater peace. This is the kind of person who writes to us about contentment, and that is why we must listen. Paul knew that he was not a prisoner of circumstances. He was free! He was rejoicing in the Lord!

Do you feel like you are a helpless victim of your circumstances? "I'm stuck living in this city, how will I ever find my spouse if they live in another city or even another country?" Do you feel trapped in your loneliness and your environment? Maybe you are already married and feel trapped in your marriage. Some people feel trapped in their bodies, discontent with their appearance. There are many things that make us feel powerless and enslaved.

Lonely And Afraid

Who likes to be alone? Julia, a 25 year old Russian girl, wrote in an e-mail, "Maybe it sounds silly, but I just don't want to be alone in the evenings, and I want to be sure in advance that somebody waits for me!" No, it is not silly. It's reasonable to want to get married and share your life with someone who truly loves you and makes going home something you look forward to. Our society tells us that having a marriage partner is the remedy for loneliness. Have you noticed this theme in most movies? "If I get married, I will share a bed with another person. We will share our meals together, experience intimate moments, discuss our dreams and share our feelings. I won't be lonely anymore!" Then why are so many married folks still lonely? How is it possible to still feel neglected when you share a life with that special person? Because being lonely is not linked to your marital status. Loneliness is something we all experience when we are separated from our Heavenly Father. We make attempts to fill this emptiness with other humans. Only when we are united with God will we be safe and secure. It's that simple.

> Then why are so many married folks still lonely?

If you aren't a genuine child of God, and are living a life of disobedience to Him, a degree of loneliness is inevitable. If, on the other hand, you have experienced the spiritual rebirth through Christ, you will begin to know God's satisfying love. Our fear of being alone can be completely overcome by receiving God's love for us. *"Such love has no fear, because perfect love expels all fear. If we are afraid, it is for fear of punishment, and this shows that we have not fully experienced his perfect love."*[36] The only way to drive out our deep-seated loneliness is to fully experience God's perfect love through Jesus Christ as our Savior. *"We know how much God loves us, and we have put our trust in his love."*[37]

God is waiting on you to trust in His love so that He can remove your fears. Let me explain how I came to trust in God's love.

Emotional Rollercoaster

For the first 19 years of my life I was ignorant about the secret of contentment. I had no idea that contentment was a by-product of knowing God personally. I needed to find God and His purpose for my life, and I didn't know where to start. Worse than that, I didn't even know I had a problem! My life revolved around me — I loved myself more than God and more than others. I would do things for others if I could get something in return. My best friends in high school shared the same interests that I had — girls, soccer, fishing, hunting, and rock and roll. I judged everyone who was different than me by making fun of the way they talked or dressed. You would not have wanted to know me! Why did I act like such a jerk? I was insecure and thought that I would feel better about myself by tearing others down. But it doesn't work that way. I was still unhappy. Actually, I felt worse, because my conscience bothered me for hurting others with my sharp tongue. I even hurt my dear parents with my sarcastic remarks and disobedience. At times, I hated my own brother and started fights with him.

I began to understand why I felt so unhappy. I noticed that when I got my own way I felt happy, and when I didn't, I was unhappy. My life was an emotional roller coaster with ups and downs. When I had a date, I felt loved and important. When I didn't, and that's the way it was during most of high school and college, I felt lonely and worthless. When I made a good grade, I felt intelligent, and when I didn't, I felt stupid. I played in one varsity soc-cer game during my first year at Clemson University and scored a goal. I will never forget the thrill I felt during this match in Brevard, North Car-olina. But the elation was short lived. The rest of the season, I sat on the bench, bored, and jealous of my best friends who got to play in the games. I was frustrated. God kindly showed me that the reason I experienced these ups and downs was because my life revolved around me. When

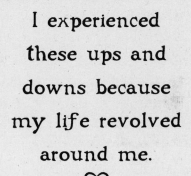

I experienced these ups and downs because my life revolved around me.

I got what I wanted, I was happy and felt important. When I did not get what I wanted, I was jealous, angry, and lonely and it made me feel worthless. I was my own god! But, the one and only God wanted to be the center of my life and take control. He showed me how much He loved me through Christ's death on the cross for me. He proved to me that I could trust Him completely and escape my roller coaster life of emptiness and guilt. He offered me a new start, a new life, if I would turn from my selfishness and give Him everything. I did just that at the beginning of my second year of college.

I can tell you that my life still has ups and downs, but they are much less dramatic. God is the source of my joy, not my circumstances. I have been learning to receive life from Him alone. This joy and contentment has grown over the years, as I learn to put my hope in God above all else. People will disappoint you, even a great spouse will let you down at times. That is why you can never put your hope in them more than God. God will never, never fail you! He will always be faithful and good to you. *"For the Scripture says, Whoever believes in Him will not be disappointed."*[38]

That's a promise you can build your life on! I have been God's child for 37 years and He has never disappointed me. I could fill an entire book with personal stories of how He has proven His goodness and faithfulness to me. Now it's your choice.

Discussion Questions
Chapter 5

1. How would you define contentment?

2. What do our circumstances have to do with contentment?

3. How does God drive out our fears?

4. Why was the author on an emotional roller coaster? Are you?

Chapter 6

WHO NEEDS A MARRIAGE CERTIFICATE?

Testing The Waters

"Why do we need to get married anyway? What good does a piece of paper do? We love each other we just want to live together. What's wrong with that? Who says we need to be married to have a good relationship? We are living together so we can see if we are compatible and then we may get married. Isn't it better to find out now before we get married?" They sound logical don't they? Maybe these thoughts resonate with you.

"My boyfriend and I have sex together because we love each other," Angela said defiantly. "It's okay, because we are going to get married!" Dozens of students, including Angela, were enjoying a lively debate. Time seemed to fly as we discussed different controversial issues. It was a "class" without walls and without rules. It was strictly voluntary; one could come and go as they pleased. On that clear spring day, the dogwood trees had the look of fresh snow as their branches were covered in white blossoms. Angela blurted out this comment during the course of our dialogue on love and marriage.

A few weeks later, I met Angela as I walked across the campus. But this time she lacked the boldness she had during our first encounter. She told me, rather sheepishly, that she had broken up with her fiancйr. I felt badly for her. She had given this guy more than sex. She had given him her heart, and now she was carrying around the broken pieces, trying to figure out what went wrong, and how to put her heart back together. I offered her hope as we spoke about God's plan for her life, His forgiveness, and healing love. Angela is an example of this popular, yet flawed, thinking. Some of this thinking is a result of watching movies and television where immorality is flaunted as the norm. Some of this thinking is the result of the painful fallout from their parents' failed marriages. The devastation they experienced firsthand makes them afraid of commitment. To avoid the same failure, they rationalize that "playing house" with their girlfriend or boyfriend is a logical alternative. It will give them a good taste of life together so they can make an informed decision. It seems safe. But, is it?

> When two people have sex together, they give a part of their soul to that person. It is an irreversible exchange.

Unfortunately, there are many flaws to this theory. When two people have sex together, they give a part of their soul to that person. It is an irreversible exchange. Sex between two humans is not the same as when two animals mate. We have a soul. God made us unique. We were created in the likeness of God with an eternal soul and the unique ability to communicate with other human beings. We have the ability to create, to reason, and to have a relationship with our Creator. When the Bible referred to Adam and Eve having sex, it says that he *knew* her. *"And Adam knew Eve his wife; and she conceived."*[39] This alludes to a deeper communication and unity of souls, not what we normally think of when we think about sex. It is an emotional and physical bonding that is only intended for one man and one woman in marriage.

God designed marriage for our mutual good, to unite and bond two lives permanently with His love, *"For this reason a man shall leave his father and his mother, and be joined to his wife; and they shall become one flesh."*[40] When two people have united physically and emotionally through sexual intercourse, separation and/or divorce is always painful. There is no way of escaping this fact. Some have described divorce like gluing two pieces of paper together, and then trying to separate them after the glue has dried. What happens? Not only is it impossible to restore them to their original state, but both pieces of paper are torn in the attempt. Severance was never part of God's loving design. He designed marriage to be a life-long commitment! *"I hate divorce,"* says the God of Israel. *"I hate the violent dismembering of the 'one flesh' of marriage." So watch yourselves. Don't let your guard down. Don't cheat."*[41] God hates divorce, because He wants us to experience the pleasure and security of a lifelong commitment.

God's desire has always been for us to be totally satisfied and committed to one another, to the point that looking outside of our marriage for another mate is unnecessary and foolish. Adultery, and all sex outside of the marriage covenant, is a perversion of the original design and the desire of our loving Father.

Haunted by Reruns

Most of us are romantically or physically involved with someone before we get married. This involvement can range from a simple close friendship or date, to full-blown sexual intercourse, like Angela and her fiancйr. Our mind makes a video every time we become romantically or physically involved with someone of the opposite sex. Cool eh? No, not really. The video tapes of past relationships will be played again and again in your mind after you are married. Is that something you want to live with? I can emphatically tell you, "No! It can kill a marriage!" Marriage is challenging enough without having to deal with your past. Satan will attempt to destroy your marriage by replaying past relationships in your mind. He hates you and anything that brings true joy and satisfaction. Jesus Christ said this about Satan, *"The thief's purpose is to steal and kill and destroy. My purpose is to give them a rich and satisfying life."*[42] Satan may tempt you to long for a past relationship and live in a fantasy world, especially when you are having difficulty in your marriage. The problem is that you can't go back. You remember what it was like when you were single. Your life was less complicated, and you experienced that "awesome romance." You may have been living at home or in the dorms, and mom and dad were paying all the bills. Now you are married, have two children, and work fifty hours a week. Your responsibilities are stressing you out. Life seems tough. It is easy to want to escape to these past relationships when life was great, or so it seemed. Was it really better? Or, were you simply immature and time made these memories seem perfect? Be careful, we can all deceive ourselves. We must follow God's truth to avoid the deception and the consequent disaster. Let's see how.

Your past relationships can haunt you with tremendous guilt. Maybe you got your girlfriend pregnant, and she had an abortion, or gave birth to your child. You must free yourself from past failure and guilt or they will kill you and your marriage. The feelings of guilt are there for a reason, usually a good one. You are guilty before God! Ouch! You have done something that God says is wrong and you feel bad inside. This is the Holy Spirit convicting you. Listen to Him. He is trying to get you to turn away from immoral thoughts and actions, and experience His forgiveness and subsequent freedom. Jesus said to the Jews who had trusted Him, *"If you hold to my teaching, you are really my disciples. Then you will know the truth, and the truth will set you free."*[43] Only the truth, the truth of Christ, can set us free. No other religious leader died for your sins. He alone is God and the Savior of the world. This can be a hard pill to swallow for our ego. We are all proud and self-righteous which makes it difficult to admit our sins and failures. The Jews responded arrogantly to Jesus and were blind to their own sins, *"They answered him, 'We are Abraham's descendants and have never been slaves of anyone. How can you say that we shall be set free?' Jesus replied, 'I tell you the truth, everyone who sins is a slave to sin.'"*[44] The self-righteous Jews found it impossible to agree with Jesus that they were slaves. They were slaves to sin — pride, lust, and greed. So was I.

Sometimes we get mad at God when He points out our sins. We may think that He is the Cosmic Killjoy who takes pleasure in our misery. But, God's only motive is our good! His motive is pure freedom from selfishness and judgment is His loving desire for you.

Angry At Your Doctor

Let's imagine that you went to your doctor because of a recent growth on your face. Your friends convinced you to visit the doctor and make sure it was not something serious. You agreed and made an appointment and the doctor took a biopsy of the growth on your cheek. He said to come back in two weeks after the lab ran some tests. You returned to his office in two weeks. Your doctor calmly said, "Please sit down. I have some bad news and some good news." First he tells you that you have a very aggressive skin cancer, "You could die in less than a year." When you hear this, you are so upset that you jump out of your seat and flatten your doctor with a right hook to his jaw, screaming in his face, "Why did you tell me that?

That ruined my day! I am going on vacation today and this is horrible. I can't believe you would be so insensitive!" I hope you would not go ballistic like this. If you sat there quietly, the next thing the doctor would have said was, "Recently a new drug was discovered for this type of cancer that is 99% effective. We think you should begin treatment immediately. And because we detected your cancer in the beginning stages, the chance of a successful treatment is even greater." At this point, you would probably jump out of your seat and hug your doctor! At least you would enthusiastically thank him and ask him when you could begin the treatment.

Many of us get angry with our spiritual Doctor -God. We get ticked off with His diagnosis, and want to punch Him out. Our pride will not let us admit that we have a spiritual cancer, one that we cannot cure. We cannot identify the illness without our loving Heavenly Doctor's expertise. *"Jesus answered them, "It is not the healthy who need a doctor, but the sick. I have not come to call the righteous, but sinners to repentance."*[45] He points out our illnesses, and in the very next breath, He tells us that He is the cure. He took our sin in His body to give us life. It is like God chose to have a transfusion and took all of our cancer cells and gave us His cancer-free blood. That is what Jesus did when He died on the cross for you and me.

In the same way that you trust your doctor with your health, you can trust God in matters of relationships. While the doctor knows what is best for your body, God knows what is best for your whole life! God wants you to be committed to your spouse for a lifetime and to be faithful to them for a reason. He is trying to protect you, and others, from unnecessary pain. Listen to your Heavenly Father's heart, *"Give honor to marriage, and remain faithful to one another in marriage. God will surely judge people who are immoral and those who commit adultery."*[46] God is strongly opposed to immorality and adultery because He loves us and cares about our wellbeing!

An Alternative To Marriage

My friend Susanne has lived with her boyfriend for a few years now. We met on a plane during one of my mission trips to Russia. She was returning home to Europe from a trip to Disneyworld with her family. We shared a similar passion for running and decided to keep in touch, hoping we would meet again. I am always thankful for the opportunity to speak to anyone who is interested in spiritual matters. God's love motivates me to share with others how they too can experience Him. I wanted to tell Susanne about my best friend, Jesus.

Over the next few months, we corresponded and I asked God to reveal Himself to her. Then, about a year later, Susanne met the members of our mission team for dinner, during a forced layover in her city. A few years later, her family graciously invited my son and me to visit them. They were hospitable and treated us like kings. She took us on a scenic run along the river that flowed through her picturesque city. Later I had the privilege of sitting down with Susanne, and explaining how she could know God personally. We had a very good conversation at her kitchen table, but like so many, Susanne believed that she could get into heaven by her good deeds.

Susanne graduated from the university a few years later and presently she is working as a nurse in a hospital. She is a compassionate person, so I know she is an excellent nurse! She moved in with her boyfriend, Jorge, shortly after going to work. Do I condemn her for this? No. Is it right? No. I believe her actions will hurt her, as we have previously discovered God's mind on this subject. I thought the same way before God opened my eyes.

God will never force us to do what is right. He will only show us the truth, appeal to our conscience, and leave the decision to us. He will reveal the danger and foolishness of our sin. Why? Because He longs for us to live free and secure in His love. God offered Suzanne this freedom from guilt and security in His unconditional love. He still wants this for her. He wants this for you. He has not given up pursuing a relationship with Suzanne. I often pray and ask God to open her eyes to this truth because I want her to find real love — in God's arms. No matter how great Jorge is, he can never provide what she desperately needs. By the way, while writing this book, I received an e-mail from Suzanne informing me they are planning to get married this year. At this point in time, Suzanne does not understand her need for asking Jesus Christ to be her Savior and Lord, but God can change that. He opened my eyes, helped me to humble myself, and respond to His mercy. He can do the same for Suzanne. He can do the same for you! Are you willing to be transformed?

Would you use your expensive laptop to hammer a nail in the wall? Only if you were crazy! Why not? It was not made for that purpose, and this action would damage it.

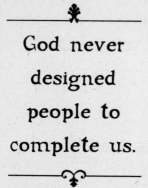

God never designed people to complete us.

You and I were made to have are relationship with God, to talk and laugh with Him. You were created to honor Him with your trust and obedience. You were fashioned to receive His love and care and then give this love to others. Marriage is an opportunity to practice this giving and receiving. When you are not rightly related to God through Jesus Christ, you are not truly fulfilled, and you are harming yourself. Your life resembles using your laptop as a hammer! Oh, to many, it may appear that you have it all together. But, when you are alone, you admit that something is missing because you feel frustrated and have no peace. If you choose to surrender control to God, then you have the potential to have healthy relationships with others. Only when we are reconnected to our Creator can we connect in marriage, the way God originally intended. I can tell you from my personal experience, surrendering control of everything to God and following His plan for marriage really works!

Vertical and Horizontal

The key to a good marriage is a solid, healthy, secure relationship with God. The vertical relationship, the one with God in heaven, is the foundation for healthy horizontal relationships. Your relationship with your spouse, children, parents, friends, boss, and every person you meet, stands or falls on your relationship with God. If you do not know God in a personal way, and daily draw life from Him, then you will attempt to find security in a person or persons. Remember the "earth-shaking" problem we discussed in chapter two. There isn't a person on the earth that can make you happy. There isn't a woman on the earth that can make a man happy! It does not matter how attractive, intelligent, funny or kind she may be. There isn't a man on the earth that can make a woman happy! It does not matter what he promises, how handsome or wealthy he is, or how hard he tries to please you! Why is this true? God never designed people to complete us. God completes us when we are united with Christ! *"So you also are complete through your union with Christ."* [47] Yes, there is a certain degree of happiness that others can give us, but they never can come close to the Creator's love and fulfillment. That is where we must start. Without the vertical relationship in good working condition, the others will never reach their potential. God is the source of love who empowers us to love and sacrificially give to others. We are ready to get married when, and only when, God is our life and our security. What if you are divorced? Is there still hope for you? Absolutely!

Discussion Questions
Chapter 6

1. "It's logical to live together before marriage and find out how compatible we are." What do you think about that reasoning?

2. What is point of the story, "Angry At Your Doctor?"

3. What is God's design to make you complete?

Chapter 7

SHOULD

I CONSIDER REMARRIAGE?

Amy's marriage was not the fairy tale romance that she had dreamed of as a little girl growing up in East Lansing, Michigan. "Marriage was my ticket to being loved and validated. I wanted to feel special to someone," she told us. "My family was very dysfunctional and I was running away from them, it didn't feel okay to be alone." Amy had been divorced for 8 years when my wife and I met her through a mutual friend. She was working endless hours as an administrator at a retail store when we met her. We wondered later on, was she a workaholic attempting to escape her past or was she trying to avoid an uncertain future?

God allowed my wife and me to befriend Amy over the next several years and she began to open up to us about the ugly details of her former marriage. She had escaped an abusive relationship, years before we met. Her first husband became heavily involved in pornography and drinking. Amy told us she finally had to move out, "When he physically abused me and threatened my life, I finally left." After one year of separation, her husband only got worse and she divorced him.

Her past still seemed to have a stranglehold on her that kept her from moving on and experiencing the full life God had planned for her. But, she informed us that she had learned some valuable lessons from the hardships of her first marriage. She understood through Christian counseling what the root problem was. She confided, "I was constantly trying to substitute a man's love for the love only the Lord could give. I didn't understand it until years later that I was really making marriage and the love of a man into an idol." She broke off an engagement to a man in her church for this very reason. Then she did not date for ten years, and was not remarried until twenty years after her first marriage dissolved. In Amy's words, "If I had known at twenty-eight that I would be single for the next twenty years, I don't think I would have handled it very well. The hardest thing was feeling lonely and unworthy of love, yet I punished myself for ten years by avoiding dating and getting hurt again. I could not see how much God loved me and wanted a relationship with me. He worked so hard to get my attention but I was stubborn. It took much heartbreak for me to realize this." Amy reasoned that it was much safer to stay single, even if it was terribly lonely. She knew that rebounding from one bad relationship into another was not what she wanted. She wanted God's best and was willing to wait for it, whatever that meant. What God wanted was her whole-hearted devotion. She cast herself into His loving arms with complete trust. In Amy's own words, "These feelings slowly gave way to surrendering my life, my dreams, my plans to God and letting Him teach me how to trust Him in spite of the pain. Especially in the hardest times He was showing me how to lean on Him and get to the point where I said, "Even if I am single the rest of my life, I trust you. I love you. You know what you are doing. My life is yours and you created me. You have a purpose for my life. You call the shots. Help me trust you.""

God revealed to Amy that being single does *not* make you a pariah. You are not a second-class citizen! It may be that the most fulfilling life, for you, is one of being single. It all boils down to knowing that God has an incredible plan for your life, one that is beyond your greatest dreams.

It is hard to trust again after you have been hurt deeply. Both partners are broken and confused after a divorce. It is hard to pick up the pieces of your life and go on. On some days, it seems impossible and you want to quit. You feel like Humpty Dumpty, nobody can put your life to-gether again!

Can Anyone Fix Humpty?

Humpty Dumpty sat on a wall;
Humpty Dumpty had a great fall.
All the king's horses, And all the king's men,
Couldn't put Humpty together again.

Humpty Dumpty is a character in a Mother Goose rhyme that most English-speaking children are familiar with. He was a large egg that was given human characteristics, although this was never stated in the rhyme. The term "humpty dumpty" was 18th century slang for a short, clumsy, or obese person. Of course, a clumsy person falling off a wall may not be irreparably damaged, whereas an egg would be. The rhyme is no longer posed as a riddle, since the answer is now so well known. The rhyme ends sadly with Humpty Dumpty so broken that the best in the business (all the king's horses and all the king's men) were perplexed by his tragedy and unable to fix him. You may feel like Humpty Dumpty after your broken marriage -shattered emotions lying on the ground, helpless and hopeless. There is good news! There is hope for you. The God of the impossible specializes in putting Humpty Dumptys back together, even better than the original! Your marriage may not be restored, but He can and will rebuild your life if you ask. He is the specialist in the field! Why not call out to God, and give Him a chance? *"Call to Me and I will answer you, and I will tell you great and mighty things, which you do not know."* [48]

It is good advice to never make a decision when you are broken and weak! You were wounded deep down in your soul by the divorce, and now you are fragile and susceptible. Wisdom says to heal first before getting involved with someone else. The pain is still fresh, placing you in a vulnerable situation. You must take the time, make the effort to heal, and become truly secure in God's love, before you think seriously about remarriage. This healing process usually takes a long time. Be patient!

Our friend Amy got married this year to a great man named Rick. She wrote to us, "I had to be completely broken and surrender my plans and dreams to God *without* expecting Him to give me what I wanted. My whole Christian life I sought the good things God gives but I didn't really want to know Him. My prayers were full of going to the

Lord and essentially saying "please do this and thanks for giving me that, I really want your good gifts but I don't really want to spend the time to know you." When God has your life, your whole life, He can, and He will, shower you with His good gifts. Take the time to meditate on this amazing promise, *"For the Lord God is our sun and our shield. He gives us grace and glory. The Lord will withhold no good thing from those who do what is right."* [49]

He is waiting on you. He wants you to seek the Giver, more than the gifts that He gives. He knows that only the Giver of life can make you secure and complete. Do you know that? Amy ended her letter with these remarks about her new husband, "My husband truly does seek to love me as Christ loves the church. He stands firm as a leader of our family, yet I see him putting my needs above his own." Amy is one more Humpty Dumpty that God miraculously put back together. She humbly asked God to change her life and then she obeyed His principles. She sought security in Christ before she got remarried.

Looking For Mr. or Ms. Right

Who will you marry? We all agree that this is one of the most important decisions in life. Okay, then why do we fail so miserably? Nobody in their right mind gets married intending to get a divorce! We all dream of "living happily ever after" with the love of our life. We focus a tremendous amount of energy on finding the right mate. When we are convinced we have done this, we make a life-long

121

commitment. We fully expect that we will succeed and experience a happy marriage filled with love and romance. We sincerely believe that our love for one another will overcome the odds, but in reality, 50% of the marriages in America end in divorce. Many other countries in the world have a similar failure rate. Why is it that often, after only a few short years of marriage, the romance has evaporated, the commitment is shattered, and we are desperate for a way out! What happened? How did we get blindsided? What didn't we see in our spouse?

> Usually we are in the hunt for "Mr. or Ms. Right" and we give little or no thought to our own preparedness.

During one of my discussions on marriage, Lynn, a college student, listened intently. She made a few brief comments every now and then, but she seemed shy and reserved. I found out later why she was withdrawn — it was the freshness of her private pain. "I divorced my husband this year. We were married for only six months," Lynn said, choking over her words. "Why, what happened?" I asked cautiously, not expecting the answer she gave me. "When we were dating, my husband was a kind and caring person. He would often bring me flowers and take me out to dinner. Immediately after our wedding, he became verbally and emotionally abusive. I was completely shocked! He was not the same person I dated." The tears in her eyes revealed the broken heart inside this young woman. Lynn's "Mr. Right" was oh so wrong! How could this happen? How could she prevent a reoccurrence? Could she ever take the risk and trust her heart to someone again?

Mr. or Ms. Ready

Marriage will always involve a certain amount of risk. Is there a way to minimize the risk? Is there is better way of finding a spouse? Maybe one should reflect on his own life first. Wow! Who has the courage to go there? I hope you do. Usually we are in the hunt for "Mr. or Ms. Right" and we give little or no thought to our own preparedness. I strongly encourage you to consider an honest self-evaluation to determine if you are "Mr. or Mrs. Ready." Are you secure with who you are to the point that you are operating your life from a position of security and strength? Are you content with being single the rest of your life? "Are you kidding?" you exclaim in disbelief. If you are not content being single, getting married is not going to make you content. If you are content and secure before you say, "I do," you have a very good probability of finding the right person for you, and for all the right reasons. More importantly, you will bring strength to the marriage relationship, and guarantee its longevity and satisfaction. Isn't that what you want? I know that I longed for this security, and by God's grace, it is what my wife and I have been experiencing for the past 34 years.

Now, at last, let's explore in detail how you can become the secure person you really want to be.

Discussion Questions
Chapter 7

1. If you are divorced, why should you risk getting hurt again? Are all men dogs? Are all women impossible to live with?

2. What does Steve want to communicate through the story of Humpty Dumpty?

3. Are you ready to get married? Why, or why not?

Chapter 8

BECOMING SECURE

Overnight Security

Becoming secure is a life-long process that takes time and effort. We can see a major transformation during our lifetime! "Where do I start?" you ask. You begin with understanding that you are broken and need help, like Humpty Dumpty. The apostle Paul understood his predicament. He embraced his weaknesses and found strength through Jesus Christ. God told Paul, *"My grace is all you need. My power works best in weakness."* Paul responded, *"So now I am glad to boast about my weaknesses, so that the power of Christ can work through me."*[50]

The first step is acknowledging your insecurity and understanding the cause. It is crucial to your healing to understand how you became the person you are today. You must also comprehend where true contentment comes from. You must know in your heart that you are separated from God and in need of a Savior to bring you back to God. A spouse can be a savior, but not the Savior! There is only one Savior who can rescue you from the insecurity caused by your guilt. This guilt is caused by choosing to disobey God which the Bible calls sin. Sin is doing what God says is wrong and breaking His commands. It is the opposite of God's perfect nature. Everyone sins. Everyone has this serious problem;

we love ourselves more than we love God and more than we love others. This selfishness separates us from God, and His love for us, thus making us insecure. That is why we have feelings of guilt when we lie, steal, lust, or get angry with others. We have offended a holy God and we are under His judgment, awaiting punishment in hell. This is eternal separation from God. This is not a pretty picture is it? But, thank God, the story does not end here!!! God intervened in history! He came to the rescue like a knight in shining armor riding on a white horse.

> **Doing good deeds won't get you into heaven. If it could, you could boast of our accomplishments.**

Jesus came down from heaven two thousand years ago to save us by dying on the cross, in our place, for our sin, to give us new life. The second step is to humbly acknowledge — I need help outside of myself. I can't fix myself. Remember, you are Humpty! My own selfishness and self-reliance is the cause of my insecurity, because they separate me from my Father and His love. I need to be rescued. The question you must answer is, "Will you ask Jesus to intervene in your history?"

The final step begins with your salvation — when you personally turn from your selfish life, asking God to forgive you, and chose to receive Jesus as your Lord and Savior. You surrender control of your life to Him. At this point you begin a life-long process of growing in God's love which will make you more and more secure. This occurs when you take steps of faith and obedience. Your personal relationship with God begins when you are saved from sin and hell. From that moment on, God wants you to grow in your relationship with Him, becoming more and more secure each day.

God s Gift is Free

A common misunderstanding is that a personal relationship with God, or what the Bible calls salvation, can be earned. I believe that many people think this way, because almost everything in life is earned or paid for in some way. If you want to have chicken for dinner tonight, you must pay someone at the store, unless you raise your own chickens. But even then, you must pay someone for the chicken feed, unless you grow your own corn. It takes money or some other commodity to trade for, or purchase, the goods and services you want. Thankfully, this principle is not true when it comes to salvation! If it were, we could not get into heaven. God says that the best we do is not enough, because our very nature is corrupt. God offers us eternal life as a free gift and we cannot obtain it by working for it. Doing good deeds won't get you into heaven. If it could, you could boast of our accomplishments. Also, there would be no need for a Savior, right? Here is how God says we come to Him for eternal security, *"For by grace you have been saved through faith; and that not of yourselves, it is the gift of God; not as a result of works, so that no one may boast."*[51] We don't deserve eternal life, because we have all sinned against a holy God. *"No one is righteous— not even one. No one is truly wise; no one is seeking God. All have turned away; all have become useless. No one does good, not a single one."*[52] God would be perfectly just to judge us for our sin. We all deserve to spend eternity suffering in hell. That is what makes His gift so astonishing. It is completely undeserved. Jesus Christ chose to take our punishment because, *"God is love!"*[53]

It is your decision whether to receive Christ or not. If you are ready to receive God's gift, by trusting Christ as your Savior and Lord, simply tell God you want to be saved. God is not as concerned that you say these exact words, as much as He is concerned about the attitude of your heart. Jesus promises to save you if you sincerely ask Him. *"Whoever will call on the name of the Lord will be saved."*[54] If this is what you truly desire, you can say these words to God.

"Dear God, I know that I am a sinner. I have lived a selfish life. I know that I deserve to go to hell. I don't want to live this way anymore. Thank you that you love me, and died on the cross for my sins. I give you the control of my life. I want Jesus to be my Savior and my Lord. Thank you for hearing my prayer, and making me your child. I ask this in Jesus' name."

Did you ask Jesus to save you? Did He hear you and answer your prayer? Of course He did! He promised! He never lies because He is God! God wants you to be absolutely certain that you are His child. This verse describes what you just did, *"If you will confess with your mouth Jesus as Lord, and believe in your heart that God raised Him from the dead, you shall be saved."*[55] Did you ask Jesus to take control of you life and become your Lord? Then He did! These promises are God's assurance for every new believer. If you called on Christ to save you, by praying the prayer above, then He did! Did you ask Him to come into your life, to forgive your sins and make you His child? Then He heard your request and He answered you. Don't overly depend on your emotions, trust God and His word, the Bible. Your feelings can mislead you. The fact is, you are His child, now and forever! This solves your main problem — the origin of your insecurity. Now you are eternally secure in Christ and His love. Congratulations!

If you are not ready to make this decision, know that God loves you personally, and will continue to seek you. Please continue to seriously consider trusting Jesus Christ as your Savior. He wants to give you real security and He alone is capable! Ask Jesus to reveal Himself to you and show you if He is real and worthy of your trust. The choice is yours.

Eternally Secure

The beautiful thing about coming to Christ for eternal life is that you belong to Him now and, well, eternally! That is why it is called *eternal life!* Nothing and nobody can separate you from Him! If you find this hard to believe, then rest assured in God's guarantee, *"God has said, "Never will I leave you; never will I forsake you." So we say with confidence, "The Lord is my helper; I will not*

What does God do when you fail? He is there to pick you back up, to remind you of His unconditional love, and to help you move forward.

be afraid. What can man do to me?""[56] It thrills me to tell brand new Christians this promise! God is the one who saved you, not yourself, and He will never lose you! Often, new Christians are afraid that they will sin, and God will leave them -they fear they will lose their salvation.

Shawn was six feet five inches tall, weighed 250 pounds and played football for Clemson University. He was rather intimidating to talk to for someone my size at the time— a skinny 6 feet 2 inches tall and 165 pounds. Hey, what do you expect? I was a soccer player! I met Shawn in the dormitory and a friendship began to develop between us. He was interested in spiritual matters, but he was hesitant about giving Jesus Christ control of his life. So I asked him, "What keeps you from trusting Christ, Shawn?" He said, "I am afraid, that if I give my life to Christ, I will sin." He was afraid he could not keep his end of the bargain. I assured him that he would sin, but that becoming a child of God was not a bargain to maintain. I assured him that salvation was a free gift that God never takes back, "Christianity is a personal relationship with God. He promised to never leave you. We don't get eternal life by our good deeds and we can't lose our salvation by our bad deeds!" Now wait a minute. I am not saying that we can sin all we want to after becoming a Christian! I went on to tell Shawn, if we are truly saved, we will not want to sin! We will want to please the God who loved us and died in our place on the cross. In addition to this motivation not to sin, we receive the Holy Spirit the moment we trust in Christ. He gives us the power necessary to obey God. Shawn was extremely relieved to hear this good news. This is what the Bible calls grace. We don't deserve God's mercy and love, but He gives it to anyone who believes in Christ. We can relax after we trust Jesus as our Savior, because He will never divorce us! He will always be with us and will always love us!

He will never leave you, even if you turn your back on Him! God loves you every moment of every day. You will remain His child, even when you sin. Our seven children are Nelsons forever, even when they disobey their mother. Why? Because they were born Nelsons! Once you are spiritually reborn into God's family, you can never be unborn! You will always have God's name. Of course, God wants you to grow spiritually: to learn how to resist temptation, to learn how to rely on the Holy Spirit's strength and not your own. The truth is, you will not obey God all the time. Nobody does. What does God do when you fail? He is there to pick you back up, to remind you of His unconditional love, and to help you move forward. Let's read about God's unchanging love.

"He who did not spare His own Son, but delivered Him over for us all, how will He not also with Him freely give us all things? Who will bring a charge against God's elect? God is the one who justifies; who is the one who condemns? Christ Jesus is He who died, yes, rather who was raised, who is at the right hand of God, who also intercedes for us. Who shall separate us from the love of Christ? Shall tribulation, or distress, or persecution, or famine, or nakedness, or peril, or sword? Just as it is written, "For Thy sake we are being put to death all day long; we were considered as sheep to be slaughtered." But in all these things we overwhelmingly conquer through Him who loved us. For I am convinced that neither death, nor life, nor angels, nor principalities, nor things present, nor things to come, nor powers, nor height, nor depth, nor any other created thing, will be able to separate us from the love of God, which is in Christ Jesus our Lord."[57]

I cannot think of a more secure place to be, can you? It is impossible for Satan and his demons to separate you from God. It is impossible for any difficulty, any hardship, or any person to pry you away from God. No sin or failure from your past can stop God from loving you. Nothing in your present or future will hinder God's compassion for you. You can't even separate yourself from God if you wanted to! This is eternal security! Secure in His love.

He saved you and *He* will never let you go. You are eternally secure in His hands, *"My sheep hear My voice, and I know them, and they follow Me; and I give eternal life to them, and they will never perish; and no one will snatch them out of My hand. My Father, who has given them to Me, is greater than all; and no one is able to snatch them out of the Father's hand."*[58] I will often picture myself in the hands of Jesus and the Father tightly holding Jesus' hands in His. I am being held by these two sets of omnipotent hands.

Growing In Security

Although you became secure when you took the step of faith in Christ as your Savior, there remains a lifetime of growing to be done. You entered this new relationship by faith, and now God wants you to continue by faith, *"And now, just as you accepted Christ Jesus as your Lord, you must continue to follow him. Let your roots grow down into him, and let your lives be built on him. Then your faith will grow strong in the truth you were taught, and you will overflow with thankfulness."*[59] You will experience God's love as you learn to rely on Him, depend on His word, and get help from other members of God's family.

There are dozens of good books to help the new Christian grow in faith. You should also find a good church and faithful Christians who will gladly help you grow more secure in Christ. It is good to learn your weaknesses and Satan's lies so that you can win the battle in your mind. Anyone can fall. I know Christian leaders who have turned from their wives to other lovers. Stupid? Yes! God warns us about the consequence of adultery, *"For the prostitute reduces you to a loaf of bread, and the adulteress preys upon your very life."*[60]

Then why do Christians fall? We fall into sin because we have believed a lie, and not the truth. The man believed that the prostitute would make him happy. She may have gratified him, but only for a short time. God says all sin is that way short-term pleasure and long-term pain! He wants us to understand that the pleasure from sin is short-lived, *"the passing pleasures of sin."*[61] Sin lures us in with "You can have it now," then bites us back later. God wants us to see through these lies and avoid sin! American author Henry Miller said, "In this age, which believes that there is a short cut to everything, the greatest lesson to be learned is that the most difficult way is, in the long run, the easiest." Temptation will never reveal the destructive consequences of yielding to its deceit. On the other hand, doing what God says will always be beneficial for you, and for others. God's ways are win-win! God's ways are always prudent and lead to long term security. Therefore, you must diligently study the Bible to be prepared for the lies that Satan will throw at you.

Great Searchings of Heart

And the princes of Issachar were with Deborah;
As was Issachar, so was Barak;
Into the valley they rushed at his heels;
Among the divisions of Reuben
There were great resolves of heart.
Why did you sit among the sheepfolds,
To hear the piping for the flocks?
Among the divisions of Reuben
There were great searchings of heart.[62]

Deborah was a great prophetess of God who courageously led Israel into battle against Canaan. She and Barak rallied six Israelite tribes to defeat the army of Jabin, king of the Canaanites. Why do the verses from this song say there were, "great searchings of heart?" Everyone who goes to war faces the possibility of death. They will automatically have, "great searchings of heart" as they contemplate the stark possibility of their death and their eternal destiny. There is something cleansing to the soul about staring death in the face. Nothing is more sobering than life and death situations. Every battlefield is consumed with these great searchings of heart.

The Unseen Battle

You and I are engaged in a battle. It is no less real, and no less dangerous, than one fought with swords and spears. Ours is an unseen spiritual battle with eternal consequences.

This battle takes place in every relationship and in every marriage. Therefore, every Christian must have "great searchings of heart" in order to engage and win this battle. You must learn the art of spiritual warfare to protect yourself and remain secure. How? You must identify your selfish habits, the destructive lies you have believed, and how to combat them with truth. It is our faith in God that defends us against these attacks, *"In addition to all of these, hold up the shield of faith to stop the fiery arrows of the devil."*[63] You must also learn to protect yourself from the harmful influence of certain people who seek to destroy your faith in God, and erode your security. *"He who walks with wise men will be wise, but the companion of fools will suffer harm."*[64] Are you willing to fight the spiritual battle against Satan and his followers? Do you sincerely want to grow in Christ-likeness and win the battle? Then you too must have "great resolves of heart." This means you must honestly evaluate yourself and set your will to change. This requires more strength than is humanly possible. To be secure in God and His love, you will need the Holy Spirit's help; to read and act on the Bible, to learn to pray about everything, and to depend on the support and prayers of your fellow soldiers (believers). Be patient, it is a process, and change is not always overnight. It took you years to become who you are, and it will take time to change. You have probably heard the saying, "old habits die hard." It will take time for you to develop the habit of trusting God and the Bible, more than your old selfish habits and passions. Your false securities will often put up a long hard fight before you learn how to live without them. Some egotistical habits will change more quickly than others. Some habits you will battle the rest of your life. Learn to depend on God's strength and grace to overcome.

❧

If the best plan for you is to be married, God promises to meet that need, in His timing. Nothing can stop Him!

❧

Paul encouraged Timothy, his young disciple, to be strong in God's grace, *"Timothy, my dear son, be strong through the grace that God gives you in Christ Jesus."*[65]

Remember, you are God's special work. He loved you enough to save you from hell, and He made you His child. He started this work in you, and He will finish what He began, *"And I am certain that God, who began the good work within you, will continue his work until it is finally finished on the day when Christ Jesus returns."*[66] Relax! Trust Him completely! If you are a child of God and single, you can know that He loves you dearly, and will do everything necessary to meet your needs. If the best plan for you is to be married, God promises to meet that need, in His timing. Nothing can stop Him! If it is His best for you remain single, He will give you the grace to have a life just as full and satisfying as any married person. I love what the Psalmist wrote about his security in God, *"With Your counsel You will guide me, and afterward receive me to glory. Whom have I in heaven* but You? And besides You, I desire nothing on earth. My flesh and my heart may fail, but God is the strength of my heart and my portion forever."[67] I have prayed, "Whom have I in heaven but You?" countless times to keep my heart focused on loving God. God often reminds me through these words that He *alone* is my hope, my joy, my life, my all! They are great verses to memorize to resist the temptations of loneliness, lust, and selfishness, when they come knocking at your heart. "Be prepared" is the well-known motto of the Boy Scouts and a great motto for every child of God. Be prepared for the temptations, because the battle in your mind will continue until you see Jesus Christ face to face in heaven.

God Will Be There

You will fail. You will give in to temptation and suffer temporary setbacks. Yet, you will NEVER be defeated, because Jesus won the war by dying on the cross and being raised to life. We are winners, now and forever. Learn to get back up after you fall, *"For though a righteous man falls seven times, he rises again, but the wicked are brought down by calamity."*[68] Learn to be honest with God and admit and turn from your sins. *"He who conceals his sins does not prosper, but whoever confesses and renounces them finds mercy."*[69] Learn to thank God for His love and forgiveness that never fails. Meditate on this verse, *"Because of the Lord's great love we are not consumed, for his compassions never fail. They are new every morning; great is your faithfulness."*[70]

Grace

Henry Miller's comment is profound, "the most difficult way is, in the long run, the easiest." It is difficult to resist lust, dishonesty and jealously. But, it is much easier to resist when you look at the long-term results of giving in to these sins...divorce, distrust, bitterness, guilt and increased loneliness. Doing what is right in the eyes of God will always prove to be the best for us and for others. God's way is always a win-win for everyone. There are no short-cuts to quality relationships. You will need God's grace to protect you from the deceitfulness of sin. This grace enables you to resist the "short-term gain" of lust, lying and selfishness in a relationship and pursue the "long-term gain" that comes from a secure relationship with God. A strong relationship with God results in a sacrificial love for others. God will give you grace to overcome your fears with His love. The fear of being alone, the fear of being unloved, the fear of marrying the wrong person, the fear of being stuck in a bad marriage or the fear of not having the strength to remain faithful to our spouse, can immobilize us. These fears will haunt us our entire lives if we don't learn how to let God remove them, to drive them out with His grace and omnipotent love. His perfect love will cast out your fears!

Discussion Questions

Chapter 8

1. What is the first step to becoming secure?

2. In your own words, describe how a person receives a new life from God.

3. How can God's gift be free when we have broken His laws?

4. Will God ever "divorce," or stop loving, His children?

Chapter 9

FINDING THE ONE

Quail Hunting

I am passionate about going out on a cold, frosty November day with a good, short-haired pointer in pursuit of the wily Bob White. The Bob White, or quail, is a small brown bird that lives together in groups called coveys. They are known for their speed and elusive flying ability. They have embarrassed many a grown man over the years as they darted back and forth, flying through the trees to escape. I have many fond memories of hunting in eastern North Carolina with my grandfather, Floyd Davis Turnage. I can still feel the rush that I got when the covey of birds exploded in flight under our feet, and the challenge of picking out one bird to shoot. Most of the time the birds won! I would point my shotgun in the general direction of the birds and fire. Usually, the only thing that fell was some pine needles and leaves. Fortunately for us, Granddad rarely missed. He was an excellent shot. Then my dear grandmother, Lula Marie Turnage would prepare a delicious feast of quail, along with succulent tomatoes, black eyed peas, lima beans, turnip greens, and new potatoes from their garden. Marie was the best cook I have ever known! Of course, she had the advantage of feeding a gang of starving men who had walked all day through soybean fields in Pitt County. I miss those days hunting with my brother and granddad!

When I refer to "finding the one" I'm speaking about something far more important than hunting for little birds. But, I want us to think about how we pursue what is valuable to us. I have always enjoyed hunting, whether it was for candy Easter eggs as a child, or for someone's lost ring. Recently, I helped a lady in our water aerobics class find her ring. She accidentally dropped it in the pool, and I eagerly joined in the search for the lost ring. It was something of value to this lady, and therefore worth searching for. This is who I am. I am a hunter by design.

I think God built this hunting instinct into all men. For women, this drive to find something of value is called "shopping." Okay, that was a joke! As a young man, I was excited by the adventure of "hunting" for a girlfriend! When I got older and more serious about finding a marriage partner, I realized that I was out of my league. I was not equipped for this search. There were many times when I felt frustrated, and the hunt lost its aura. The emotional obstacles seemed insurmountable, and there was too much about women, love, and marriage that I did not understand. I needed divine intervention to succeed, and that is what I got. I realized that God was God, and that meant He knew everything and everyone. He loved me dearly, and He could help me find my partner.

Where to Begin

I really hope you will evaluate yourself first to see if you are ready. Are you secure, content with who you are, to the point that you are operating your life from a position of security and strength? You must "get your own house in order," before you can truly be of use to others. The writer of Psalms prayed this, "Search me, O God, and know my heart; test me *and know my anxious thoughts. Point out anything in me that offends you, and lead me along the path of everlasting life.*"[71]

I still had tremendous insecurities that took time to change, even after I gave my life to Christ. By God's grace, I grew in my relationship with Him, and experienced His love in practical ways. Still, I continued to believe that I needed a wife to make me complete. It took several years before I was truly content being single. There were many bumps along the road, most of which were self-inflicted, as I got over my insecurities and fears. Here is one of my self-inflicted bumps.

I almost married the wrong person! Yes, I was a new Christian, so was Denise. We dated for a while and became close friends. We were both young Christians and enjoyed helping one another grow in our new faith. After some time, I became convinced that God wanted us to be husband and wife. I asked her to marry me, telling her I was convinced that it was God's will. She did not agree, and we eventually went our separate ways. What happened? How could I have been strongly convinced, and yet so wrong? I had prayed a great deal about this matter, studied the Bible to find God's will for this decision, and I had asked other Christian friends for advice. The problem was my heart! *"The human heart is the most deceitful of all things, and desperately wicked. Who really knows how bad it is?"*[72] I wanted to get married so much that I deceived myself. I was desperate! I had not let God overcome my insecurities to the point where I was totally satisfied with Him. I thank God that He protected us and our future spouses! I know that God was gracious to us, and that He answered our prayers for His will. Watch out! You too can fool yourself. You too can manipulate others and get what you want. You could end up with a marriage partner

You can not have two kings ruling in one kingdom!

that you so desperately want, but not the one for you! (Let me caution you here. If you are married, you are married to the right person, unless there is abuse or adultery involved. This subject requires more discussion, and would take another book to do it justice.) Even if you are a true believer in Christ, you can be deceived when it comes to choosing your marriage partner. Is God in control of everything? Yes! I think God has only one person for you. But, you have a free will that God will not violate. You still have a selfish nature that wants to deceive you and control you. How can we avoid self-deception?

Your Isaac

Can you imagine how difficult it would be to sacrifice your son? I can't! My wife and I have two wonderful sons whom we love dearly. It would be the most difficult situation I could ever imagine. Listen to what God asked the Jewish patriarch Abraham. "Then God said, *"Take your son, your only son, Isaac, **whom you love**, and go to the region of Moriah. Sacrifice him there as a burnt offering on one of the mountains I will tell you about.*"[73] God promised Abraham that his descendants would be like the sands of the sea. At the time God made this promise, Abraham was ninety-nine and Sarah, his wife, was eighty-nine years old. It would have to be a miraculous conception. Isaac was born when Abraham was one-hundred and his wife Sarah was ninety, far beyond their child-bearing years!

Then God tested Abraham to see whom he loved more, his God or his precious son Isaac. God told Abraham to take the son of his dreams and go sacrifice him. That seems crazy doesn't it? Here's what happened, *"Abraham took the wood for the burnt offering and placed it on his son Isaac, and he himself carried the fire and the knife. As the two of them went on together, Isaac spoke up and said to his father Abraham, "Father?" "Yes, my son?" Abraham replied. "The fire and wood are here," Isaac said, "but where is the lamb for the burnt offering?" Abraham answered, "God himself will provide the lamb for the burnt offering, my son." And the two of them went on together. When they reached the place God had told him about, Abraham built an altar there and arranged the wood on it. He bound his son Isaac and laid him on the altar, on top of the wood. Then he reached out his hand and took the knife to slay his son. But the angel of the Lord called out*

*to him from heaven, "Abraham! Abraham!" "Here I am,"
he replied. "Do not lay a hand on the boy," he said. "Do
not do anything to him. Now I know that you fear God,
because you have not withheld from me your son, your
only son.""*[74] God knew that Abraham was willing to do
anything He asked. He wanted *Abraham* to know it. He
wanted him to under-stand that we never truly have something until we are willing to give it away.

The only way to find God's perfect will for your life is to
surrender yourself and every decision to Him. Whatever
decision you are contemplating — who to marry, what car
to buy, how to raise your teenager, or how to invest your
money-fully yielding to God's loving leadership is where
you must begin. You must put your Isaac on the altar! Tell
God you will do anything He asks you to do, and then He
will show you. *"If anyone is willing to do His will, he
will know of the teaching, whether it is of God or whether
I speak from Myself."*[75] It is essential to be willing to do
whatever God tells you before He reveals it. Tell Him that
you are willing to do whatever He tells you, even if this
means not marrying a specific person you are strongly attracted to. If you are not willing, ask Him to make you
willing. Ask Him to remind you of His love that He proved
on the cross. He promised to supply all of your needs —
let Him do that and don't take matters into your own
hands. If we struggle with being willing to do what He tells
us, it is usually because we have turned our eyes away from
the cross and His amazing love. Only when you are broken
and willing to do anything He shows you, are you in a po-

sition to be led. Give the person you are interested in to God. Give every decision to Him. Finding your spouse starts with a healthy respect for God. He will gladly lead you, if you are willing to follow.

Honest Friends

Another essential ingredient in finding your mate God's way is to ask other Christians to pray for you to know God's will, and to give you their honest advice — not just tell you what you want to hear. You say that you don't have any friends like that? Then ask God to give you some, and try to be this kind of person to others. Then, read the word of God and listen to what He is telling you. He wants you to take the truth of the Bible and apply it to your situation. There are principles that He wants to use to guide you. For example, one way to know if God is leading is through your motives. God tells us to not do anything from self-

He wanted him to understand that we never truly have something until we are willing to give it away.

ishness or pride, *"Do nothing out of selfish ambition or vain conceit, but in humility consider others better than yourselves. Each of you should look not only to your own interests, but also to the interests of others."*[76] Ask God to reveal your true motive in the relationship, knowing you can deceive yourself. *"The human heart is the most deceitful of all things, and desperately wicked. Who really knows how bad it is? But I, the Lord, search all hearts and examine secret motives."*[77] If there is hidden selfishness, ask God make it known to you. He will! Don't be afraid. He only has your best in mind! You must be convinced of this.

Practical Suggestions

1. Pray. Ask God to show you His will, and to make you willing to do it, no matter what He shows you. Pray for humility to listen to the advice of your friends. Ask God to help you consider your potential mate as being more important than yourself. Ask Him to protect you from self-deception and selfish desires, and to give you moral self-control.

2. Get Counsel. Seek out mature friends and ask them to give you an honest assessment of your relationship with this potential mate. Make sure your potential spouse is around your friends enough for them to get a good read on this person, and observe how the two of you relate.

3. Listen to God. God speaks to us through the Bible. Read it daily with an open heart and mind because, *"the word of God is alive and powerful. It is sharper than the sharpest two-edged sword, cutting between soul and spirit, between joint and marrow. It exposes our innermost thoughts and desires."*[78] In other words, God's

word reveals our true motives and helps us understand the difference between our plans and His. Ask God to help you apply His truth to your life and your relationship. Reading the Bible is worthless if you don't apply it, "Now that you know these things, you will be blessed if you do them."79 Jesus promised to bless us if we obey.

4. Be patient. Take it slowly. Don't make a rash decision. *"Love is patient."*[80] If either partner is impatient about getting married, take this as a signal to seriously evaluate the relationship. Impatience is selfish and reveals insecurity that must be dealt with before marriage. People can often say whatever the other partner wants to hear, because they don't want the relationship to end.

5. Listen to your potential mate. They may be sending you a signal that they need more time to decide. Remember, that love *"does not demand its own way."*[81] If you are demanding and pushy, you can force something that may not be God's plan or timing. Ask your partner to tell you if you are pushy.

6. Discuss the hard issues. Be honest with one another about your strengths and weaknesses. The fewer surprises you can have after your vows, the better. Talk honestly and openly about past relationships, money, children, life-goals, values, relationships with your in-laws and careers. Talk candidly about what place God and your church will play in your lives.

7. Premarital Counseling. When you get engaged, I strongly recommend premarital counseling. I also suggest that this person be a real Christian and a mature follower of Christ. A third party can be impartial and help you both see any blind spots or weaknesses before marriage. They should use the Bible as the foundation of their counsel.

Unequally Yoked

Katia was a Ukrainian woman in her early twenties, living under intense pressure to get married. Katia felt this relentless stress from her parents and peers to find a husband before it was too late. Therefore, when a friend and I were discussing with Katia how to trust God with this area of her life, you could sense her struggle. I will never forget our conversation as we sat at a restaurant on Khreschatyk Street in the heart of Kiev. Katia resisted the idea of trusting this precious area of her life to her new-found God. She had only known Christ for a short time. She had seen Him change her life in many ways, but this was a major test of her young faith. When we discussed the subject of marriage, Katia was dating a non-Christian. We showed her this passage from the Bible about a Christian and a non-Christian getting married.

"Do not be yoked together with unbelievers. For what do righteousness and wickedness have in common? Or what fellowship can light have with darkness? What harmony is there between Christ and Belial? What does a believer have in common with an unbeliever? What agreement is there between the temple of God and idols? For we are the tem-

ple of the living God. As God has said: "I will live with them and walk among them, and I will be their God, and they will be my people. Therefore come out from them and be separate, says the Lord. Touch no unclean thing, and I will receive you. I will be a Father to you, and you will be my sons and daughters, says the Lord Almighty." [82]

Katia bristled when we encouraged her to consider breaking off this relationship. She responded with, "I would rather marry an unbeliever than not be married at all." "Katia, I really think it would be a mistake!" I replied. "I have counseled many couples where one partner is a believer and the other is

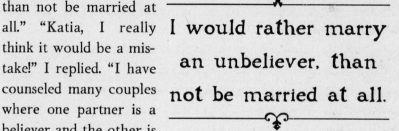

I would rather marry an unbeliever, than not be married at all.

not. They have serious conflicts in their relationship because they have a different purpose and different values." We told her that her unbelieving boyfriend would never be able to love her as much as she needed. He did not have the ability to do so, even if he wanted to, because true love only originates with God, *"Dear friends, let us love one another, for love comes from God. Everyone who loves has been born of God and knows God."* [83] He did not have the Holy Spirit to empower him with the sacrificial love she was looking for, and that God wanted her to experience in marriage. Why was she willing to compromise and settle for something less than God's best? Katia was operating her life from a position of weakness and insecurity. She had this young man, and did

157

not want to let him go. She feared being alone more than she trusted God and His love for her. Many of us can relate to Katia, I know I can, especially with such a major decision.

Are you more afraid of being alone than you are of trusting God completely with your future spouse? Are you presently dating an unbeliever? Do you know what God says about these relationships? I know it is difficult to surrender this person to God, but He will give you the strength if you ask Him.

I love to go fishing, any kind of fishing! I guess it's like hunting in water. When I go trout fishing, I will often use a mesh bag to hold the fish that I have caught. When I catch a fish, I gently place the fish in this bag. I keep the bag in the cold, flowing water so the fish will stay alive. If I catch a bigger fish, I will often let one of the smaller fish go. But, I never let a fish go until I have a bigger one to replace it. That would be irrational!

Trusting God with your unbelieving boyfriend or girlfriend is like throwing all of your small fish back in the river before you have caught a bigger fish! It may seem foolish, but it is a wise step of faith, a step of faith in God and His unfailing love. Most fishermen fear going home without any fish. It's called "being skunked" in the fishing world. One of the greatest fears that we all share is being alone! It is a powerful fear that can cause us to act contrary to God's plan for our lives. Are you aware of this fear in your life and its effect on you?

A Mother's Advice

"The sayings of King Lemuel contain this message, which his mother taught him."[84]

Who is better qualified to give a son advice about finding a wife than his own mother? Of course, a father's input is very important too. A father can offer insight and perspective that a mother will not have; whereas, a mother understands certain aspects about women that are invaluable. A wise son will give serious consideration to her counsel - after all, she too is a woman! She understands how women think, act, and feel. She is aware of their unique needs. We will look at one wise mother's advice to her son as he faced the daunting task of choosing his wife.

It is difficult to authenticate who this mother and her son were. Ancient Jewish tradition says that she was Bathsheba, the queen of Israel, and that her son was King Solomon. He is referred to as King Lemuel in this proverb. We can confidently say that this proverb is a mother's advice, divinely inspired by God, which has withstood the test of time. These enduring truths have impacted millions of marriages over the centuries in every culture. My wife and I can testify to their power and positive effect in our marriage.

Other Gods

It was paramount for the king to make a wise, calculated decision about his bride — for his own life, as well as for

159

the nation. The Israelites were God's people, and therefore they needed their king to have a marriage that honored God, and one every couple could imitate. His mother's first instruction was a warning, *"Do not give your strength to women, or your ways to that which destroys kings."*[85] Sadly, King Solomon did not listen to his mother's wise counsel, and his kingdom was destroyed. He foolishly chose to have 700 wives and 300 concubines, most of whom had other gods. They severely impacted his life, turning his heart away from the one and only God.

"Now King Solomon loved many foreign women. Besides Pharaoh's daughter, he married women from Moab, Ammon, Edom, Sidon, and from among the Hittites. The LORD had clearly instructed the people of Israel, 'You must not marry them, because they will turn your hearts to their gods.' Yet Solomon insisted on loving them anyway. He had 700 wives of royal birth and 300 concubines. And in fact, they did turn his heart away from the LORD. In Solomon's old age, they turned his heart to worship other gods instead of being completely faithful to the LORD his God, as his father, David, had been."[86]

This principle is still true for single men today. If you are a genuine Christian man, and choose to marry a woman who is not, then she will probably turn your heart away from God. The prudent action is to wait on your loving Father to bring you the woman He designed specifically for you. She will be someone who obviously loves Jesus and others. Wait on God's best, and don't take matters into your own hands. God wants your wife to be your biggest blessing, not your biggest burden! Prayerfully, let Him lead you every step of the way. If you are convinced that you should marry a woman who loves Jesus, why would you even date anyone who was not a Christian? What did the King's mother tell him to look for in a potential wife? (Ladies, of course these principles are true for you too.)

Trust

The first quality she told her son to look for in a woman was trustworthiness. Find a woman who has a track record of reliability, especially in stressful situations. Her example of dependable service to others will inspire you to serve God. This special woman is someone you can depend on to be loyal to you during hardship and trials. She will be faithful her entire life, *"Who can find a virtuous and capable wife? She is more precious than rubies. Her husband can trust her, and she will greatly enrich his life. She brings him good, not harm, all the days of her life."*[87] This honorable woman will demonstrate self-sacrificial love for others long before you consider marrying her. It is her true character, and your entering the picture does not make her act like someone she's not. Her love for others will be evident to all, not just you. If it is not, throw her back!

This is why I am not a big fan of dating. Dating is a game we play where two people do their best to impress the other person. Openness, honesty, and trust are essential for a good marriage. But it all goes back to how secure

I am. If I am secure in God's love, then I will be satisfied with how he made me -how I look, my background, and my personality. I will be myself — real, open, and honest. I will not try to hide my weaknesses or faults. These are the ingredients for trust in a relationship. Our godly mother instructed her son to look for a virtuous woman— a woman who helps him love God. That does not mean she has to be the most mature Christian woman in the world. It means that God has designed one specific

> **Dating is a game we play where two people do their best to impress the other person.**

woman for one specific man, who has the potential to build his faith more than any other woman. I don't believe there are five, ten or a hundred women that will work as well. Why not? It is my personal opinion, that our sovereign, loving God has one specific person just for you. It seems obvious to me that the King's mother believed this too, and that is why she helped him know what to look for. He was looking for his soul mate that God had fashioned only for him.

This wise mother also told her son that appearance can be misleading. I can imagine her saying, "Watch out! Be careful, son. Do not let a woman's appearance deceive you!" She said, *"Charm is deceptive, and beauty is fleeting."*[88] And this advice came from one of the most beautiful women of that time! Notice, she did not say that beauty was evil. She simply instructed her son not to be led by his eyes, not to overemphasize beauty. Beauty does not last. It can be a trap. Many a man has fallen into this trap and been severely injured!

Signals

What signals are you sending to others of the opposite sex? I can see that you are probably scratching your head and saying, "What are you talking about? How do I send signals to the opposite sex?" We all send messages to others, and most of them are non-verbal. Are you aware that you communicate by:

- how you dress
- how you speak to others -parents, friends, teachers, your boss
- what kind of movies and television shows you watch
- what books and magazines you read
- what music you listen to
- how you spend your money
- how you spend your time
- what body language you use

These signals reveal what kind of person you really are. They tell others how much you think you are worth. If you dress modestly, you are telling others you are valuable.

You are telling the world of singles that you are not cheap. You will not "sell yourself" to just anyone who makes an offer. You are worth a lot to God! He, the King of the Universe, died for you! Remember that. *Your* King died for *you*! How much does that make you worth?

Ladies, do you wear provocative clothes that say, "Look at me!"? Why? You are looking for someone to love you and think you are beautiful. Instead, you will have men chasing you so that they can simply get you into bed. This is a reality, and most young women are clueless about the signals they are sending. They naively imitate what they see on television and in the movies. They need a loving father and mother to explain to them the reality of how men think. Often, young men are immature, and allow their emotions and passions to control them, not thinking through the numerous consequences of sex outside of marriage. Actually, they don't think most of the time! They react to what they see. If you want them to focus on what you look like, then spend hours and hours on your appearance, and a lot of money on your clothes, and only a little time on your character. If you choose this lifestyle, men will miss the real you! They will think that you don't value yourself. There is much more to you than your body. Yes, God gave you your body, and He did an awesome job! But, it is not the most important part of who you are. If you ask God, He will help you send the right signals to men -signals that will attract a man of integrity who will value you for the princess that you are! What is a woman's highest quality?

A Woman s Highest Quality

The King's mother closes this instruction with the grand finale'. She tells her son the highest quality a woman can have. What is this pearl her son should discern in a potential wife? In her own words, *"Charm is deceptive, and beauty is fleeting; but a woman who fears the LORD is to be praised."*[89] By all means, find a woman who fears God! This does not mean she is afraid of God, but that she wants to honor and obey Him in all that she does. She honors God by trusting Him to show her what to do in every decision, and with every area of her life. This is a rare quality in a woman (or in a man). God is not simply an attachment to her life — an appendage. God is her life! She is secure in God's love for her, and that is what motivates this beautiful woman. Appreciate and praise this woman! Respect her. Her worth is far above jewels!

Men, as you search for your wife, make your top priority finding a woman who fears God. Don't sell yourself short. Don't settle for just, "a Christian woman who attends church." Let God bring you a woman who lives to please her Creator. You want a wife who demonstrates her genuine love for others every day. Find out what kind of character she has *before* you consider a serious relationship. You too are of great value. Hold out for the best! Remember, love is patient. God will not disappoint you. If it is His will that you get married, read and heed this wise advice from the King's mother. It's God's advice.

Illusion or Reality

Sabrina had to face her fears and their impact on her heart. She was the main character in the popular romantic movie,

---

Illusions are dangerous, they have no flaws. You seem to be embarrassed by loneliness, by being alone. It is only a place to start.

Sabrina, whose fear of being alone and unloved almost ruined her life. *Sabrina* grew up near the Larrabee mansion on Long Island. Her father was employed as the chauffer for the wealthy Larrabee family. As a young girl, she often fantasized that David Larrabee was her imaginary lover. David was one of the wealthy Larrabee sons who Sabrina constantly dreamed about marrying one day. But, David had never noticed this young girl. He was a shallow playboy who was so self-absorbed with a different girlfriend every week that he never noticed this young girl's affection.

Sabrina's father finally convinced her to go to Paris to find herself. She went, and there she began to work for a photographer. Her employer had a heart-to-heart talk with Sabrina over lunch. The woman knew Sabrina was "in love" with a man back in New York. She made the wise comment about David, "Illusions are dangerous, they have no flaws. You seem to be embarrassed by loneliness, by being alone. It is only a place to start."[90] We are often embarrassed to admit we are lonely, and we despise this state of existence. The embarrassment we feel because of our loneliness drives us to create dangerous fantasies. We fall in love with the idea of being in love. We create relational illusions to make us feel better, only to suffer the pain of reality later on. The reality, which we have covered earlier in this book, is that no person can satisfy us. Only our Creator can give us life! He so deeply wants to do so!

It is not easy being single! I finally grew in God's love enough to become secure and content in my singleness. Only then was I prepared to be married. It was several years after I came to know God before I allowed Him to bring me to this place - the place of being at peace as a single person. After this difficult growth process, in early 1975, I realized that Danelle Patricia O'Toole was the one God had designed for me. How did I know? Danelle helped me love Jesus Christ more than any other woman I had ever known! The first thing that attracted me to her was her love and commitment to Jesus Christ. She was content in His love. She was growing in her relationship with God daily. By the way, I was not strongly attracted to her physically until after I noticed her true worth — her love for God. That was the opposite of every other woman I had considered as a wife before that time. I am not saying that this should be the rule, but it was a good sign for me. It verified to me that this relationship had the right priorities.

Then I began to see how beautiful Danelle was physically. In reality, she was physically attractive all along. I think God was doing a work in my heart to help me mature, and to be able to recognize the greatest beauty a woman can possess.

The second characteristic that got my attention was how Danelle cheerfully served other people in our church. I could see Jesus Christ living in her by her deeds, and that was attractive! Another reason I chose to marry Danelle was to help her as well. I saw her respond to my leadership. God was using me to build her faith and she communicated this fact to me. She was my perfect match. After 34 years of marriage and raising seven children, she is still my soul mate, my love and my best friend!

There is nothing on earth compared to the adventure of walking with the living God and experiencing His unchanging love! He longs to reveal this love to you in surprising ways every day. One of these will be the area of marriage. God has a specific someone for you too, if it is His will that you get married. Wait for Him.

Discussion Questions
Chapter 9

1. Steve admitted that he almost married the wrong person! Why?

2. What vital lesson must we learn from the story of Abraham and his son Isaac?

3. What "Isaacs" do you need to put on the altar?

4. Discuss the Practical Suggestions with your friends.

5. Why should Christians only marry Christians? What is your opinion?

6. Why do people date? How successful is this model of courtship?

7. What signals have you been sending the opposite sex?

RECEIVING LIFE FROM GOD

This illustration represents the idea that a strong, satisfying marriage is one where both partners receive life from God and give of themselves to one another. Both the husband and wife have a personal relationship with God where they draw strength from Him to love each other. He is the source of their love, the motivation to serve one another and the power to act Christ-like in marriage.

The following covenants are for you to seriously consider. They are written for singles who want to be prepared for marriage; to be the person they need to be before marriage, so that they can be the person they want to be in marriage. It is a covenant between you and God. It is not for anyone else. If these words express the desires of your heart, I suggest that you ask God to make this a reality in your life. Ask Him to help you keep this covenant and to grow in His love to the point that you are ready for marriage. Then, sign it as your way of showing God how serious you are about following His plan for marriage. You may want to cut Your Marriage Covenant out of the book. Then, put it in an envelope and save it in a safe place, as tangible evidence of the covenant between you and God. Or, you may want to frame it, so that you can be reminded of His love and your commitment to Him and marriage. Please note, the first covenant is for a woman and the second one is for a man.

I hope that the principles contained in this book have been helpful to you and your future marriage. If you are already married, I hope that applying these truths to your relationship will make it stronger and more secure. Please contact me if you have any questions.

Secure in God's love,

Steve Nelson
Kiev, Ukraine
secureingod@gmail.com

My Marriage Covenant

Because I found true security in Jesus Christ...
He satisfies my deepest needs. He loved me first and gave Himself for me on the cross. Because He loved me in this way, I want to please Him with my life, my marriage, my all.
I have surrendered control of my life to Jesus Christ.
I have been made whole in Him.

I understand that God never created a man to complete me. Only He can do that. I will not settle for the first opportunity of marriage simply because I am afraid there won't be others. I will examine the character of a potential marriage partner over a period of time, especially in difficult situations. I will look deeper than his outward appearance and promises of love. I will wait patiently for the person God wants to give me. I will think and not just feel. I will seek the counsel of mature friends. I will say "no" to those who pursue me but who lack godly character and genuine sacrificial love.

"God, help me overcome my selfishness and become a woman who will respect and honor her husband. Prepare me to be a godly wife — one who lays down her own desires and plans for her husband. I will consider his needs as more important than my own. I can only do this by relying on the Holy Spirit."

Signed _____

Date _____

"Since he did not spare even his own Son but gave him up for us all, won't he also give us everything else?" Romans 8:32 NLB

"But seek first his kingdom and his righteousness, and all these things will be given to you as well." Matthew 6:33 NIV

My Marriage Covenant

Because I found true security in Jesus Christ...
He satisfies my deepest needs. He loved me first and gave Him-
self for me on the cross. Because He loved me in this way, I
want to please Him with my life, my marriage, my all.
I have surrendered control of my life to Jesus Christ.
I have been made whole in Him.

I understand that God never created a woman to complete
me. Only He can do that. I will not settle for the first opportunity of marriage simply because I am afraid there won't be
others. I will examine the character of a potential marriage
partner over a period of time, especially in difficult situations.
I will look deeper than her outward appearance and promises
of love. I will wait patiently for the person God wants to give
me. I will think and not just feel. I will seek the counsel of
mature friends. I will say "no" to those who pursue me but
who lack godly character and genuine sacrificial love.
"God, overcome my selfishness and help me to treat all
women with respect and honor. Prepare me to be a godly husband — one who lays down his own desires and plans for his
wife. I will consider her needs as more important than my own.
I can only do this by relying on the Holy Spirit."

Signed _____

Date _____

"Since he did not spare even his own Son but gave him up for us all, won't he also give us everything else?" Romans 8:32 NLB

"But seek first his kingdom and his righteousness, and all these things will be given to you as well." Matthew 6:33 NIV

Discussion Questions
Chapter 10

1. How has your understanding of marriage changed after reading this book?

2. What are some of the benefits of making a commitment?

3. Are you ready to commitment yourself and your marriage partner to God? Why, or why not?

Notes

Chapter 2
1. Proverbs 30:21-23 NASB
2. Psalm 73:25, 26 NLT
3. 1 Corinthians 13:4-7 NLT

Chapter 3
4. Proverbs 11:22 NIV
5. Romans 8:32 NLT
6. John 8:32 NIV
7. Micah 7:18 NASB
8. Luke 9:23 NLT
9. Luke 9:24 NLT
10. Matthew 6:33 NLT
11. John 17:23 NLT
12. 1 Corinthians 10:13 NASB
13. 1 Samuel 16:7 NASB
14. Ecclesiastes 5:3 NASB
15. 1 Peter 2:6 AB.

Chapter 4
16. 1 Samuel 15:24 NASB
17. 1 John 4:18 NLT
18. Galatians 3:5 NASB
19. Proverbs 13:20 TM
20. Isaiah 26:3 NLT
21. Proverbs 23:5 NASB

Chapter 5
22. Isaiah 30:15 NLT
23. Philippians 4:11 NASB
24. Chariots of Fire, written by W. J. Weatherby, 1981, page 150
25. Ibid page 150
26. Ibid page 65
27. James 3:16 NIV
28. 2 Corinthians 5:8 NASB
29. Romans 14:19 NASB
30. 1 Corinthians 2:9 NLT
31. Proverbs 27:20 NLT
32. Proverbs 15:13 NASB
33. Philippians 4:11-13 NASB
34. Philippians 1:12-14 NASB
35. Philippians 4:4 NASB
36. 1 John 4:18, 19 NLT
37. 1 John 4:16 NLT
38. Romans 10:11 NASB

Chapter 6
39. Genesis 4:1 KJV
40. Genesis 2:24 NASB
41. Malachi 2:16 TM
42. John 10:10 NLT

43. John 8:31 NIV
44. John 8:33-34 NIV
45. Luke 5:31-32 NIV
46. Hebrews 13:4 NLB
47. Colossians 2:10 NLT

Chapter 7
48. Jeremiah 33:3 NASB
49. Psalm 84:11 NLT

Chapeter 8
50. 2 Corinthians 12:9 NLT
51. Ephesians 2:8-9 NASB
52. Romans 3:10-12 NLT
53. 1 John 4:8 NASB
54. Romans 10:13 NASB
55. Romans 10:9 NASB
56. Hebrews 13:5-6 NIV
57. Romans 8:35-39 NASB
58. John 10:27-29 NASB
59. Colossians 2:6,7 NLT
60. Proverbs 6:26 NIV
61. Hebrews 11:25 NASB
62. Judges 5:15-16 NASB
63. Ephesians 6:16 NLT
64. Proverbs 13:20 NASB
65. 2 Timothy 2:1 NLT
66. Philippians 1:6 NLT

67. Psalm 73:24-26
68. Proverbs 24:16 NIV
69. Proverbs 28:13 NIV
70. Lamentations 3:22-23 NIV

Chapter 9
71. Psalm 139: 23-24 NLT
72. Jeremiah 17:9 NLB
73. Genesis 22:2 NIV
74. Genesis 22:6-12 NIV
75. John 7:17 NASB
76. Philippians 2:3-4 NLB
77. Jeremiah 17:9-10 NLT
78. Hebrews 4:12 NLT
79. John 13:17 NIV
80. 1 Corinthians 13:4 NIV
81. 1 Corinthians 13:5 NLT
82. 2 Corinthians 6:14-18
83. 1 John 4:7 NIV
84. Proverbs 31:1 NLT
85. Proverbs 31:3 NLT
86. 1 Kings 11:1-5 NLT
87. Proverbs 31:10-12 NLT
88. Proverbs 31:30 NIV
89. Proverbs 31:30 NIV
90. Sabrina Fair, written by Samuel A. Taylor, 1953